BAPTISM AND YOU

Baptism and You

ROB WARNER

KINGSWAY PUBLICATIONS
EASTBOURNE

ISBN 0 85476 772 X

Published by
KINGSWAY PUBLICATIONS
Lottbridge Drove, Eastbourne, BN23 6NT, England.
E-mail: books@kingsway.co.uk

Designed and produced for the publishers by
Bookprint Creative Services,
P.O. Box 827, BN21 3YJ, England.
Printed in Great Britain.

Dedication

To our fellow travellers in Kairos – church from scratch

'It's church, but not as we know it.'

We've only just begun . . .

Contents

Introduction

Your baptism can be one of the most wonderful days in your life and an enormously important milestone in your Christian discipleship. Outwardly, you declare your faith in Jesus Christ, believing that when he died, he died for you. Inwardly, the Holy Spirit can write the meaning of baptism deep upon your heart. Everyone present will be rejoicing with you, thrilled that you are declaring and demonstrating your faith in the public way that Jesus appointed for his followers. Full-blooded, New Testament baptism is the baptism of believers who are committed to living as Jesus' disciples. Because we have chosen to put Jesus first in our lives, we come to be baptized in his name.

My own baptism as a believer was thanks to the Anglican Church. I was converted, filled with the Spirit and called to full-time ministry in an Anglican setting. Like many English people, I was almost oblivious to any church except the Church of England and the Roman Catholic Church. I had hardly had any contact at all with churches that baptize believers.

When I began completing application forms for theological college, I decided to read *The Book of Common Prayer* and the Thirty-nine Articles. As I looked into the liturgy of infant baptism and the catechism, I suddenly realized that I did not believe a word of it. Because the Anglican Church was the only one I had known, I had gone along with such things, turning a blind eye. But if I was going to enter the ordained ministry, integrity required me to be fully persuaded by my denomination's practices. Reading *The Book of Common Prayer* took me back to the Bible. And I came to the conclusion that the New Testament is crystal clear. For the first Christians the crucial factor in baptizing people was not their age – whether infants or adults – but the fact that they had become professing Christians. Baptism in the New Testament is always and exclusively baptism for believers.

I had no idea in those days that there are far more Baptists than Anglicans in the world. Twenty years later it is much more widely known that the fastest growing churches in the world are Pentecostal, and they are also planting more churches in the UK than any other denomination. And they too baptize believers. The New Churches, still small in numbers but high profile in Britain, also baptize believers. And the same is true of most of the indigenous churches now springing up across Africa, Asia and South America. Many European churches have been greatly influenced in recent years by John Wimber and the Vineyard churches and by Bill Hybels and the Willow Creek model of seeker services. And both Vineyard and Willow Creek are also committed to believers' baptism. If the last fifteen hundred years have been the era of christendom, state churches and infant baptism, a new age of believers' baptism has now dawned.

This world context provides a wake-up call to Western Europe. We live in countries where infant baptism has been the standard practice for generations. Some of us have been conditioned to look down upon believer-baptizing churches as if they are a peculiar minority, with no real impact and no biblical basis for their practices. Such attitudes merely reveal our ignorance. Around the world, an ever increasing percentage of Christians have been baptized as believers. Watch out, Europe, the Baptists and Pentecostals are coming!

This book is written for four groups of people.

1. *For those planning to be baptized soon*, my prayer is that this book will help prepare you.
2. *For those who want to find out more about baptism*, my desire is that this book will make the case and explain the meaning of baptism as clearly as possible. I want to encourage you to take the biblical plunge!
3. *For those who have already been baptized as believers*, my aim is that this book will help you understand more fully the significance of baptism and its continued impact upon your daily discipleship. Discovering the riches of the New Testament teaching is really important whether you were baptized a month, a year or 30 years ago.
4. *For those with the privilege of helping to prepare others for baptism*, my hope is that this book will enrich the input you can offer.

I anticipate that this book will be used in three ways:

- It will be read by individuals.
- It will be used as a basis for a series of talks.
- It will be studied in groups, chapter by chapter.

I hope that, in addition to groups specifically preparing for baptism, some churches may see the value of studying this material in home groups. The New Testament teaching on baptism is so rich and rewarding, all Christians can benefit from exploring it more fully and applying it to our lives. I know that I have been greatly enriched by the opportunity to spend time exploring this teaching again while I have been writing this book.

I have the privilege of speaking in many denominational settings, often being asked to provide biblical expositions and leadership training. Christian unity requires us to respect one another and to work together for the glory of Christ, even when we disagree. This book is written to make a persuasive and thoroughly biblical case for the meaning and practice of believers' baptism. But there is not the slightest desire on my part to enter into or promote foolish controversy. I therefore encourage my readers to avoid engaging in any pointless knockabout and point-scoring. Should you get into conversation with those who disagree with you about baptism, whatever your convictions, listen to their case graciously and refuse to compromise your essential Christian unity. If they get heated, cool them off with a patient and generous response. The temptation to break fellowship must be resisted: we must learn to disagree agreeably, seeking always to preserve our unity in one faith, one Lord and one Spirit.

My thanks, as ever, go to my dear wife, Claire, for her remarkable support, and to my admirable sons, James and Tom. Claire and I were baptized together, which is a great experience for any married couple. In addition, I am so thankful to God for the wonderful fellowship that we enjoy as part of Kairos – church from scratch.

This introduction ends with a request. If you get baptized after reading this book, I would love to receive a photograph of your baptism. You can do this by snail mail to the publisher or electronically to Kairos at:
Kairos-cfs@bigfoot.com

Rob Warner

PART 1

Baptism and You

1

Reasons to Be Baptized

Jesus was baptized

The best possible reason for believers' baptism is simply this: Jesus was baptized. He had been circumcised as an infant in the standard Jewish way, but as an adult he was determined to mark his dedication to God's service by this public act of commitment. Circumcision was something his family had done for him. But his baptism was a voluntary act of obedience. No one compelled him – it was something he wanted to do before God on his own account.

John tried to prevent him. One of the hallmarks of a great leader is that you don't think too highly of yourself. And John was clear that he was completely unworthy even to contemplate baptizing his cousin Jesus. More than that, he could not understand why Jesus should want to be baptized in the first place. Since John was calling people to a baptism of repentance and purification, it seemed to him that Jesus was the last person in the world who needed to respond. Previously John had turned away Jewish religious leaders who were not showing signs of genuine repentance, but now he resisted Jesus' request because Jesus had no need to repent at all (Matthew 3:14).

When Jesus insisted, John complied. We don't know how many John baptized in those years, but this must surely have been the most extraordinary and unforgettable baptism in which he ever took part. As Jesus resurfaced from the river, water streaming from his head and clothes, he enjoyed an unprecedented encounter with God, when the Holy Spirit descended upon him in the form of a dove. John later explained that God had revealed to him how to identify the Promised One: the Holy Spirit would come down upon him and remain with him in a decisive, new way (John 1:33).

Full Christian baptism has a richer significance than the baptisms John performed. But his message is still important for us. For John, baptism was mainly about two things. It was a *baptism of repentance*, a decision to turn away from self-centred living and a re-dedication to living in God's way. It was also a *baptism of preparation*, getting ready for the imminent day of the Lord, the coming of the Promised One who would baptize not just with water, but with the Holy Spirit.

These two emphases remain important in Christian baptism. Everyone who is baptized as a believer certainly needs to express repentance and a new dedication to live for God. Baptism is never a reward for the saintly. Rather, it is an immersion for the undeserving, for those who are receiving the free gift of the salvation that comes from God. Baptism is also a response to the day of the Lord: we respond with faith to the coming of Christ on the pages of human history, his death and resurrection; we respond with faith that today is the continuing day of God's favour, since the saving power of the cross of Christ has no expiry date this side of the end of time; and we respond with faith in anticipation of a glorious future, when Christ finally returns and brings sin and death to their decisive end.

Jesus explained to John that his reasons for being baptized were different from any other candidate. There was no need for Jesus to repent, because he was the unique God-man, fully human yet without sin. And there was obviously no need for the Promised One to prepare for his own coming. Instead, Jesus chose to be baptized in order to 'fulfil all righteousness' (Matthew 3:15).

This 'fulfilment of righteousness' has two dimensions. First, Jesus is expressing obedience to God, since John's call to baptism was inspired by the Holy Spirit. Jesus' baptism is a clear sign of his eagerness to comply with God's every demand upon his life. Second, Jesus is demonstrating his unreserved and wholehearted identification with the human race. Rather than setting himself apart in sinless superiority, he takes his stand with sinners. In identifying with us, Jesus becomes representative of humanity. His baptism points not towards his own sins, but to his willingness to embrace his role as sacrificial substitute, the sin-bearer for the human race. At the dawn of his years of public ministry, his baptism unambiguously demonstrates the wholehearted and unreserved identification with sinners that is fundamental to Jesus' ministry. This representative role will find its fullest expression at the cross, where Jesus pays the ultimate price on our behalf: 'God made him who had no sin to be sin for us, so that in him we might become the righteousness of God' (2 Corinthians 5:21).

In accepting John's baptism, Jesus invites his followers also to be baptized. If the sinless One was willing to embrace a baptism of repentance, how much more do we need to express our repentance in baptism, when our lives are profoundly contaminated by selfish instincts. If the Promised One was willing to embrace the baptism of preparation, how much more do we need to express in baptism our willingness to accept his gift of grace by being baptized in his name. The very fact of Jesus' baptism is bound to inspire his followers to a similar baptism of repentance and faith. If it was good enough for Jesus, it's good enough for me.

More than that, if Jesus was willing to demonstrate his unreserved obedience to God by being baptized, we also need to be baptized in order to fulfil all righteousness. Baptism doesn't make me a better Christian, but it does demonstrate my willingness to be obedient in all things, in order to 'fulfil all righteousness'.

Jesus was willing to identify with sinners by embracing the baptism of John. Even so, in baptism we not only accept the inescapable and blunt truth that we really are sinners; we also choose to identify with Jesus, in both his baptism and his cross. Since the Saviour identified with sinners by being baptized, is it too much to ask that sinners identify with the Saviour by following him into the waters of baptism? Surely not. To be baptized as a believer is an act of worship and thanksgiving towards Jesus Christ, baptized and crucified for our sake. It is an act of obedience in which we follow his example. And it is an act of identification in which we stand alongside the Saviour who, even when faced with the cost of the cross, was willing to make his stand as the sinners' friend.

Jesus taught baptism

Early in Jesus' ministry, his disciples baptized his new followers (John 4:1–2). But the most important way in which

Jesus promoted baptism is found in the Great Commission. And this instruction is clearly meant to be put into practice by every succeeding generation of Jesus' followers:

> 'All authority in heaven and on earth has been given to me. Therefore go and make disciples of all nations, baptising them in the name of the Father and of the Son and of the Holy Spirit, and teaching them to obey everything I have commanded you. And surely I am with you always, to the very end of the age.' (Matthew 28:18–20)

Three times Jesus emphasizes the totality of his saving lordship. He has been given *all* authority. His followers need to go among *all* peoples. And new followers need to be taught to keep *all* that Jesus has commanded. Baptism is in the threefold name of God – Father, Son and Holy Spirit. While Luke reports that the first Christians baptized and prayed for healing specifically in the name of Jesus, Matthew emphasizes the larger context of the Trinity, with explicit mention of the Father whom Jesus revealed and the Spirit who is poured out by the Father and the Son.

A third threesome in the Great Commission tends to be obscured in English translations. The instruction to 'make disciples' translates a single word which in Greek is a verb in the imperative. That means it is a direct and unambiguous command. Just as Jesus called people to become his followers, the church should continue with the same task. The church is therefore meant to be a community that always remains open to outsiders. Whenever the church turns in upon itself as a club for the converted, we turn our backs upon Jesus' marching orders for his followers. Attached to this imperative is the third threesome of the Great

Commission: going, baptizing and teaching. These tasks sum up the three phases of making disciples. They are not included as tentative suggestions or optional extras, but take on the same authoritative weight as the main verb. This means that Jesus commanded his disciples to go, to baptize and to teach.

The command 'to go' shows that the followers of Jesus are called always to be a missionary church. The explanation that this is to 'all peoples' emphasizes that the church has a responsibility to include every ethnic group on an equal basis. The Jews are certainly not excluded by this command, but the same offer of salvation by faith in Christ can now be made to all, irrespective of their ethnic origin.

The command 'to teach' emphasizes the enduring importance of Jesus' words. And because his teaching is to be obeyed, literally 'kept', merely theoretical instruction is not good enough – it must be applied. True discipleship must necessarily and always take us from initial profession of faith into a lifestyle that is centred upon the imitation of Christ. We have to put Jesus' teaching into practice, even as he did.

The command 'to baptize' is equally strong and clear. And its place in the development of discipleship is made plain. Before the main command – make disciples – is reached, the Christians must first *go* to all nations. They were not meant to hang around in Jerusalem waiting for all nations to come to them. After the main instruction to *make disciples*, there follow the subsidiary commands to *baptize* and *teach* all things. The natural meaning of the text is plain. First we need to go. Then we need to make disciples. Once new converts have been made, we need to baptize them without undue delay. And then we must continue to teach these new disciples, helping them to enter fully into the life of discipleship. Since the Great Commission is a part of Jesus' teaching, these new disciples also need to be taught to play their part in the continuing task of making ever more disciples. To be a disciple-making church requires us to take practical steps to keep on growing, both in quality – by growing deeper as disciples – and in quantity – by adding new disciples.

The timing of baptism is very clear in Jesus' command. It should not be delayed until the end of life, waiting to the last moment in order to cram in as much practical discipleship teaching as possible. But nor should it precede personal, saving faith. According to the order of the Great Commission, once we have made disciples, it is time for them to be baptized. To force baptism upon anyone, whether at swordpoint like the Spanish conquistadores in South America or through emotional pressure, would be a grotesque caricature of Jesus' teaching. Just as his first disciples made a free choice to follow Jesus, so we, in obedience to the Great Commission, are called to invite a free response of personal faith. And this is the only qualification necessary for someone to be baptized as a believer.

Two further strands of the Great Commission set a larger context for baptism. First, Jesus promises his continued presence. The Holy Spirit has rightly been described as the presence of Jesus in Jesus' absence. He makes God continually available to the followers of Jesus, who as a result are not left bereft by Jesus' death and ascension. Second, Jesus promises his presence to 'the end of the age'. Baptism in the name of Jesus is not only an act that looks back to his death and resurrection and a personal decision to become his disciple. It also includes an expectation of the future consummation of all the promises of God. Our lives in the here and now can be shaped by this glorious future hope. We live by faith not by sight, in expectancy not fear. We set our confidence not in our present circumstances, nor our feelings which are usually changeable, but in our sure, settled and eternal destiny in Christ.

Jesus' own baptism is surely inspiration enough for many of his followers to decide to be baptized. But if his example is not enough to persuade you on its own, we can find clear and strong promotion of baptism in Jesus' teaching as well. Once we recognize that Jesus plainly commanded the practice of baptism for new disciples, it's difficult to see any good reason to delay our response. Obedience to this command demonstrates that we are serious about following Jesus and submitting to him as Lord of our lives. Are you a disciple who has put your trust in Jesus Christ? Then it is time for you to be baptized in his name.

The apostles taught baptism

On the Day of Pentecost, the church was born into mission. The Holy Spirit came upon the believers when they were gathered in private, and at once he swept them into the public arena, praising God in the streets of Jerusalem. The miracles of Jesus had provoked a double response. Some were drawn towards living faith, while others sneered, explaining his miracles away, and plotting for Jesus' execution. In a similar way, some were astonished at the way Galilean fishermen were suddenly praising God in so many languages, while others made fun of them, suggesting that they were out of their minds with alcohol, even though it was only nine o'clock in the morning.

What followed was the first of many remarkable sermons preached by Peter. At the end of his message, the people were cut to the heart and pleaded for advice as to what they should do next. Peter's reply was simple: 'Repent and be baptised, every one of you, in the name of Jesus Christ for the forgiveness of your sins. And you will receive the gift of the Holy Spirit' (Acts 2:38).

There are four clear elements to Peter's response, which sum up the New Testament teaching about Christian initiation. His hearers need to *repent*, turning away from self-centred living. They need to *be baptized* in the name of Jesus for forgiveness of sin. They need to *receive the promised gift of the Holy Spirit*. And these three things can only come about through *personal faith in Jesus Christ*. Any suggestion that the mere act of being baptized could in itself secure salvation for unbelievers is quite alien to Peter's teaching. Similarly, there is no suggestion that the church could have faith on behalf of an unbeliever about to be baptized. Personal faith in Christ is the only basis for Christian repentance and Christian baptism, and only upon those who have come to faith in him will the risen Christ pour out the Holy Spirit. Faith must come first.

Luke reports that the opportunity to be baptized was immediately made available to the 3,000 who had 'accepted' Peter's message. That is, personal saving faith makes anyone eligible for Christian baptism. Once they are baptized, Luke describes these new converts as 'added to their number'. In other words, to the four elements of Christian initiation mentioned by Peter – repentance, faith, water baptism and receiving the Spirit – Luke adds a fifth, which is *joining the church*.

When Peter preached to Cornelius and his companions

(Acts 10), he seems to have been a reluctant evangelist. He began by explaining that, as a good Jew, he should not be visiting a Gentile household (Acts 10:28). This is not exactly the most obvious way to win friends and influence people! However, before Peter got to the end of his message, something astonishing happened. Suddenly the Holy Spirit came upon the Gentiles, and they began speaking in tongues and praising God (Acts 10:44–46). This is the first recorded instance in the history of the church that God's Spirit interrupted a sermon. Luke does not give us any reasons; he simply records the facts. Maybe Peter was preaching so powerfully that there was no need for him to spell out how to respond to the risen Christ. Or maybe Peter was plodding through his message laboriously, quite unaware that Cornelius and his friends were keen to become Christians, so the Holy Spirit finally lost patience with Peter's ramblings and decided to speed things up. No doubt some congregations would be pleased if God decided to work this way more often!

Peter had visited Cornelius' house with some fellow Jewish Christians, and they quickly drew the conclusion that this unexpected outpouring of the Holy Spirit could only mean one thing. What they had witnessed was a kind of Gentile Pentecost, for the Gentiles had indisputably received the Spirit freely and abundantly – 'just as we have' (Acts 10:47). For the Spirit to be given in this way demonstrated unambiguously that these Gentiles had already become disciples of Jesus Christ, making a genuine response of repentance and faith. Since God had given them 'the same gift as he gave us, who believed in the Lord Jesus Christ', Peter and his team realized that there was no reasonable justification to prevent these first Gentile converts being baptized with water. Luke reports that Peter therefore 'ordered that they be baptised in the name of Jesus Christ' (Acts 10:48).

Peter not only commends the practice of baptizing new Christians, he considers it an obligation. The new converts are expected to submit to baptism without delay, obeying the clear command of the risen Christ. And the church is obliged to baptize all believers, irrespective of their ethnic background, social standing or gender. We stand on common ground: all need to come to personal, saving faith in Jesus Christ; all can receive the gift of the Holy Spirit; and all should be baptized as believers. Peter was so committed to the practice of baptism that he didn't make a tentative suggestion. Luke reports that he gave orders for the baptisms to take place.

We live in a world where no one likes to be told what to do. As turn-of-the-millennium Westerners, we prefer to make up our own minds, in our own time. While we would instinctively resist having baptism imposed upon us, we need to recognize how seriously it was taught and practised by Peter and the other apostles. This is no optional extra for those Christians who are particularly keen on lots of water. While baptism is the least important of the five dimensions of Christian beginnings, it is integral to the teaching of Christ and his apostles. We need to make disciples in all five dimensions.

- Turn in repentance from selfish living.
- Come to Christ in faith.
- Receive the Holy Spirit.
- Join the church.
- Give expression to our new life by being baptized, just like the first believers.

Every believer was baptized

When Paul wrote to the Romans he had not yet met them. But he took it for granted that they had been baptized as believers: ' . . . all of us who were baptised into Christ Jesus were baptised into his death' (Romans 6:3). The baptism of new believers was not a distinctive emphasis of an unusual sort of Christian. It was part of the standard practice of the early churches. This awareness of a standard baptismal practice underlined Paul's confident description of Christian unity when he wrote to the Ephesians that, just as there is one faith and one Lord, one body, one Spirit and one hope, there is also one baptism (Ephesians 4:4–6), a privilege which all believers were clearly expected to share.

Just as Paul can affirm the universal privilege of baptism among the churches to whom he writes, Luke does not report in the book of Acts a single instance of someone coming to faith who is not then baptized. There is never in the New Testament the suggestion that a new disciple should await specific, personal guidance before agreeing to be baptized. Once you were converted, it was time for baptism. Every believer, in every church, was automatically baptized.

The most striking example of baptism without delay is the Ethiopian eunuch in Acts 8. Walking a desert road at the prompting of the Holy Spirit, Philip gets into conversation with a man reading Isaiah 53. The Ethiopian is clearly an active God-seeker, who cannot understand the meaning of Isaiah's prophecy of the suffering servant. Philip seizes the moment to present the good news, and the Ethiopian is converted.

There is no time for the new convert to meet other Christians. He is due home where he is responsible for the

Ethiopian queen's treasury. As Philip continues to ride in the Ethiopian chariot – the ancient equivalent of a government limousine – they notice a stretch of water beside the road. At once they get down from the chariot and Philip baptizes him. And then the Ethiopian continues on his journey home, rejoicing in his new-found faith, while Philip continues his evangelistic ministry. Although the normal pattern is for baptism to take place in the presence of other believers, it is clearly more important for the Ethiopian to be baptized than for this pattern to be followed inflexibly. The pressures of the official's work schedule do not make him exempt from the obligation and blessing of baptism.

There were no exceptions. Everyone was baptized as a believer. Circumcision, the sign of inclusion in the Old Covenant, had been reserved for Jewish men. But neither race, nor gender, nor social standing, nor previous religious convictions were considered good reasons to make any exceptions from the universal practice of baptism. When you became a disciple of Jesus Christ, it was time to be baptized.

In Acts 19 Paul visits Ephesus, and a group of twelve men introduce themselves as fellow disciples. Paul asks them a question far too blunt for many Christians today: 'Did you receive the Holy Spirit when you believed?' (Acts 19:2). Maybe he was unsure whether they really were fully fledged disciples of Christ. Or maybe Paul was checking whether there was a similar need to that faced by Peter and John among the first Samaritan converts, who came to faith and were baptized in water, but experienced a delay in receiving the Holy Spirit until the Jerusalem apostles arrived (Acts 8). This 'Samaritan Pentecost', by the way, provides absolutely no biblical legitimacy at all for the much later rite of

episcopal confirmation. Scholars today widely agree that
there is no precedent at all for this in the pages of the New
Testament. The best explanation of events in Samaria is
that the Holy Spirit was preserving the unity of the
church and preventing old rivalries between the Jews and
Samaritans resulting in independent, national churches – a
church of the Jews and a church of Samaria.

The Ephesians' ignorance about the Holy Spirit leads
Paul to a second question: 'Then what baptism did you
receive?' (Acts 19:3). Once they explain that they have only
known John's baptism, their position is clear. The first
Christians were careful to respect John and his ministry, but
his baptism, while good in itself, was no more than a preparation for the coming of Jesus. Paul therefore explains that
this preparatory baptism of repentance needs to be built
upon by faith in the One whose coming John had foretold;
that is, Jesus Christ. The eager but untaught Ephesians are
keen to go the whole way, and readily decide to become
Christian believers. As a result, Paul baptizes them in the
name of Jesus. He then completes their full Christian initiation by prayer with the laying on of hands, with the result
that the Spirit comes upon them and they speak in tongues
and prophesy (Acts 19:5–7).

Paul's policy is quite clear. Whenever someone becomes a
Christian, it's time for them to be baptized. There are no
exceptions. The natural next step for new believers is always
baptism. Paul's approach is entirely consistent with Peter
and John's visit to Samaria. The Samaritan believers were
not baptized by the apostles because they had already been
genuine converts at the time of their baptism by Philip.
Their problem was specifically that they had not yet come
into the fullness of the Holy Spirit. Paul was ready to bap-

tize the Ephesians because this was their first opportunity to be baptized since coming to saving faith.

Just as there are no exceptions to the practice of baptizing every new believer, there are also no instances in the New Testament of rebaptism. Once you had been baptized, the visit to your town of another Christian leader did not mean that he was entitled to baptize you again. Believers' baptism is once for all.

Catherine had been baptized in the name of the Father, Son and Holy Spirit after coming to faith in a church in Nigeria. When she started coming to our church in London she asked whether she needed to be baptized again. 'Certainly not!' I replied. 'Once you have been baptized as a believer, there's no need for a repeat immersion in water.' Of course, if Catherine's previous baptism had been before she became a Christian, it would not have conformed to New Testament practice, and so I would have encouraged her to be baptized as a believer as soon as possible.

So is it a rebaptism if we baptize as a believer someone who was baptized as an infant? Paul's treatment of the Ephesians shows us the way. Full Christian baptism, according to the apostolic pattern, is for believers only, and follows on from personal profession of faith. However well intended, any kind of rite of initiation that is imposed upon someone before they have come to faith is less than New Testament baptism. Paul did not rebaptize the Ephesians; he took them through the full pattern of Christian initiation, including believers' baptism, for the first time. In the same way, when I was baptized as a believer, more than 20 years after being christened as a baby, I was not being rebaptized. I was being baptized according to the pattern of the New Testament for the first and only time in my life.

In this chapter we have looked at the New Testament reasons to be baptized.

1. Jesus was baptized in order to identify with the human race in our fallenness. Now we have the opportunity to identify with him in the salvation he has won for us, by following his example and being baptized.

2. In the Great Commission Jesus instructed his followers to make disciples and then baptize them. We demonstrate that we are taking the lordship of Jesus seriously by obeying his command and submitting to baptism once we have been born again.

3. The first Christians taught baptism as one of the key steps for new believers to take. Jews and Gentiles, slaves and free, women and men, all were united in the same saving faith, the same Holy Spirit and the same practice of baptism for every new disciple.

4. There were no exceptions. Whatever previous 'baptisms' or other religious initiations they may have experienced, every single Christian was baptized as a believer. And we should do the same.

2

Making Sense of Baptism

It's a bath

There's nothing quite like a bath! As a teenager I stayed with my grandparents one term while my parents were between houses. Each Wednesday afternoon meant rugby, and I knew that when I got home, my granny would have a hot bath running. Showers can get you just as clean, but there's something special about lying flat out in a bath. Game after bruising game the steaming gallons always did the trick, soothing the war wounds of the playing field and refreshing me for the evening of homework ahead.

Another bath that worked wonders was needed when one of our sons was playing in his grandparents' back garden. They had a pond at the time (though as a result of this little episode they had it filled in), and our three-year-old was happily playing a game that involved charging around at full speed, as most games do at that age. Suddenly he decided on the variant of rushing backwards. It was one of those moments when you can see what is going to happen, but it's too late to prevent it. There wasn't much water in the pond at the time, but there was plenty of weed and gunge. Out he struggled rather wet, even more messy and extremely smelly! In fact, he was so smelly that we couldn't let him into the house without an initial hosing down. Once the worst was off him, he was ready for the perfect cure – being plunged by Mum into a deep, warm bath. Whether or not you have been a rugby player or a pond-tumbler you surely must agree: there's nothing quite like a bath!

Baptism is not much like a long, lazy bath. You get in, get a good soaking, and almost at once it's time to get out. Yet there is a striking similarity. In the days before showers, many people had a bath once or twice a week. In between they washed rather less thoroughly than most of us do today. Bath time was when you got clean all over, thoroughly scrubbed and spotless. A baptismal pool doesn't just look like an outsize tub, it really does represent a kind of spiritual bath.

Jewish baths

The Jews in the time of Jesus were thoroughly familiar with the idea that a physical bath can have a spiritual meaning. When a Gentile family wanted to follow the Jewish faith, the males were circumcised and then each family member was immersed in water. This spiritual bath was a sign of the start of a new life among the people of God.

A Gentile was only washed in this way once. And there were strict rules to ensure absolute immersion; any kind of clothing or hair-style that would prevent everything getting wet was strictly forbidden. (This kind of legalism finds its parallel today in the misplaced fears sometimes voiced as to whether a baptism is 'proper' if not every portion of the anatomy is submerged at the same time in the case of a convert who is particularly tall or particularly round! Don't worry. It's the symbolic meaning of the physical bath, not the water itself, that really matters.)

I haven't come across many modern-day legalists quite so concerned with two other Jewish requirements for proselyte baptism: the rules said the water should, if at all possible, be 'living', that is running, and what's more cold. An open-air baptism at a local river can be an extremely powerful witness – so long as it doesn't endanger the health of the participants. Maybe some kinds of legalism find it rather difficult to survive in the British climate!

As well as this once-for-all baptism, the Jews made use of a second kind of spiritual bath. Once a year, before Passover, a ritual bath was taken as a sign of being spiritually prepared for the great feast in every Jewish home. Once this bath had been taken, you were ready for Passover, although you still needed to take part in ritual hand-washing during the ceremonies.

A third kind of spiritual bath was rather more exclusive. This wasn't a bath for every Jew or for every Gentile entering the faith. Among the Jews there was a community based at Qumran who were dedicated to holy living. To enter the community you needed to have a ritual bath. For the community members there was also a ritual bath every day. The meaning of these ritual baths was simple: a sign of being spiritually purified before God. Some community members took sin so seriously they decided that once a day was not enough. No meal was complete without a fresh purifying bath of repentance to wash away the latest contamination of sin. Three times a day was their well-washed way.

You may feel relieved not to have been a member of this zealous community. After all, a spiritual bath three times a day, or even once a day, can seem rather obsessive. Most of us would have no hesitation in dismissing such behaviour out of hand as obviously eccentric and extreme. And yet these rather soggy Jews had undoubtedly grasped a grain of truth. They had a profound sense of the holiness of God and of the reality and regularity of human sin. They knew well that not a day went by when their lives were not tarnished by sin, whether in thought or action.

We do well to learn from these Jews' grasp of the seriousness of sin. We drift all too easily into self-centred living. What's more, sin is not a once in a lifetime lapse or an occasional error that lets us down. Selfishness is deeply engrained in human character. It's built into us as fundamentally as our DNA. Not a day passes without our demonstrating some kind of selfishness, however trivial. Whenever we go with the flow, making moral choices on automatic pilot, we have a tendency to indulge our selfish instincts.

The trouble is that all these daily baths could not add up to a definite and lasting salvation. Like someone working in a nuclear power plant who has to go through a decontamination process at the end of every work-shift, these dedicated Jews had to keep coming back for another cleansing, another detoxification. The intentions of these three-times-a-day bathers were serious and dedicated. Their lives were very intense, very wet, but ultimately unfulfilling. They could never find a breakthrough to a confident declaration that the old had gone and a new start with God had really arrived.

There is a wonderful contrast between the endless repetition of their baths and the once-for-all act of Christian baptism. Yes indeed God is holy. Yes indeed our lives are profoundly stained by sin. So why are we baptized only once? Because our baptism is not only an act of repentance and a cry to God for mercy, it is also a glorious celebration of the most decisive event of history – the sacrifice of Christ, once for all, sufficient to deal with every stain of sin. The real power of Christian baptism is found not in the water but in the shed blood of Christ that brings about deep and lasting inward purification.

A dip, not a sprinkle

The Jewish experience of spiritual baths points to two key truths they recognized: the stain of sin which mars every individual; and the need for spiritual cleansing to become acceptable before God. John the Baptist preached tirelessly and uncompromisingly about the need for repentance as he prepared the way for the promised Messiah. As a public sign of repentance, he urged people to be baptized in the River Jordan. They would stride out into the water to meet John, and he would plunge them beneath its surface. The experience must have been both sombre and very exciting. Sombre, because John took life very seriously indeed and called others to join him in serving God wholeheartedly. Exciting, because this quick dip in the Jordan was the symbol of a fresh start in life. Jews who were baptized by John declared in their public drenching an absolute determination to turn their backs on their old life, and make a new start with God.

Today we use the word 'baptism' almost exclusively to refer to a distinctively religious or Christian ceremony. But for the Greeks, it was just another word for a lot of water. It was a word that could mean to dip, to immerse, to sink, to drown, to bathe, to drench, to overwhelm, to plunge, or to soak. You could be 'baptized' by debts, disaster or sadness, by exhaustion or by drink. The great tragedian Euripides used *bapto* for water splashing into a ship, but if the ship was thoroughly waterlogged and sinking, then he would use *baptizo*: it took a lot of water before anything or anyone could be said to have been baptized.

The first Christians drew both on their Jewish background and on the common Greek language of the Roman Empire. From this double background, we can see the basis of their thinking about baptism. Their teaching grew out of the Jewish idea of a bath that symbolized spiritual cleansing and they combined this with use of the Greek word for being overwhelmed or immersed by water. When Ananias met Saul shortly after his sudden conversion, he described Christian baptism in a way that would be familiar to any Jew – a spiritual, symbolic bath – and used the Greek word that naturally pointed to a full immersion: 'And now what are you waiting for? Get up, *be baptised and wash your sins away*, calling on his name' (Acts 22:16, italics mine).

Searching for purity

The last 30 or 40 years have seen an accelerating boom in cosmetics. For British men in the fifties and early sixties, using deodorant was extremely radical. Then there came Henry Cooper, the great heavyweight boxer, promoting 'all over body splash'. Soon special foot deodorant followed, and now all the major stores display his and hers Christmas packs of suitable fragrances! These days there are vigorous attempts to persuade men to follow women in the arts of exfoliating and moisturizing.

We are also experiencing a steady increase in consumer demand for food that is free from additives and genetically modified ingredients. In part this comes about as a revolt against over-processing. It may also represent something more profound though more elusive: a concern to eat pure, organic, uncontaminated foods that will somehow help us get back in touch with a way of life that is natural, wholesome and pure. The irony behind this new assertiveness of consumers against the technological interventions of the food manufacturers is, sad to say, an increase in the incidence of food poisoning. A suitable cocktail of E numbers did at least keep malevolent bacteria at bay, even if the food didn't always taste very convincing!

Behind these current trends in food and hygiene there seems to be an underlying quest for inner purity of being. This can also find more neurotic expression. I recall one student facing finals. He'd been a great success directing undergraduate plays. He'd been rather less of a success at writing essays. Suddenly the great day of reckoning was before him. To be sure, he immersed himself in revision – not to mention trying to do some of the work for the first time! But something else also happened . . . he began to wash his hands. Not once or twice, but endlessly. If he went out, he washed his hands. If he picked something up, he washed his hands. If anyone brushed against him, he washed his hands. I remember this poor chap coming round to the house where I lived. Conversation was nearly impossible because every few moments he had to leave the room. Somehow in his disturbed thinking, if he washed his hands often enough he might just become truly clean.

In contrast with such obsessive concern with outward cleanliness, Jesus taught that it is not from the outside that our moral dirtiness arises, but from the deepest instincts of our inner being: 'For from within, out of your hearts, come evil thoughts, sexual immorality, theft, murder, adultery, greed, malice, deceit, lewdness, envy, slander, arrogance and

folly. All these evils come from inside and make you
"unclean"' (Mark 7:21–23 NIV Inclusive Language edition).

The power of the cross

Immersion in water can symbolize being washed clean. The
outward washing represents an inner purification. But water
alone cannot bring this about. Nor can your decision to be
baptized make you clean before God. Only Jesus Christ
could accomplish this for us, by dying on the cross. As Peter
wrote, 'You were redeemed from the empty way of life . . .
with the precious blood of Christ' (1 Peter 1:18–19). That's
why Ananias didn't just say, 'Wash your sins away,' but went
on to explain how this has become possible – by calling on
the name of the Lord (Acts 22:16). In baptism we declare
that we can be washed clean not just outwardly by means of
water, but inwardly by means of the saving power of the
cross of Christ.

Without personal faith in Jesus Christ, the act of baptism
and the amount of water count for nothing. It doesn't matter how many times you've been baptized, or in how much
water. Only the death of Christ could atone for your sin.
Only by faith in Jesus Christ can your sin be washed away.
Without personal faith in Christ, you could be baptized as
often as those Jews in the Qumran community, or by as
many different denominations as you can think of, and it
would not make a scrap of difference. You would still share
that universal need to be washed clean spiritually.

I recall a cartoon of an open baptistry with a handwrit-
ten sign floating on the surface: 'No fishing.' They are great
words, because that's what baptism signifies. Once for all,
through the cross of Christ, our sins are taken from us. It's
as if Jesus has plunged our each and every offence to the

depths of the sea and has then banned fishing – he doesn't want us raking around for ever more in things he died to free us from.

The first Christians kept an emphasis upon baptism as a kind of spiritual bath of repentance and purification. New believers were taught to come to baptism as those who knew that they were dirty and wanted to be made clean from every stain of sin. Baptism by immersion, which goes right back to the practice of the New Testament, is the fullest and finest expression of this great and glorious truth: 'My sins are washed away.'

It's a burial – and a resurrection

A spiritual bath is likely to sound quite appealing to many people. But the suggestion that we might act out our burial seems much more disturbing. Most funerals in Britain today end with a cremation. Burials tend to mean a much more direct and shocking confrontation with the finality of death. One of my grandmothers died when I was in my mid teens, and I remember vividly my grandfather on the edge of her grave. He had been profoundly deaf for years, and his wife had tirelessly looked after him. As her coffin began to be lowered gently into the earth, the terrible reality of her death came home to him. It was a foolish, impulsive, half-crazy thing to do, but he made a sudden lunge towards the open grave. If his relatives had not held him back, that frail old man would have thrown himself on top of the coffin as a last, desperate act of love. In that moment of anguish, he would rather have been buried alive than separated from his beloved wife.

Funerals are tough times. Most people feel either numb

or emotionally drained. So why on earth should the first Christians talk of baptism as a burial? The very suggestion seems too disturbing, too strange. And yet Paul makes no apology for exploring this perspective on baptism: 'We were therefore buried with him through baptism into death' (Romans 6:4).

The symbolism is not forced. To be immersed in water is really quite similar to being buried in the earth, and Christian baptism does mark with finality the end of an old way of life. Such imagery could be applied to a simple baptism of repentance, like John's – in immersion we leave the past behind. But Paul uses death and burial imagery to bring us into direct contact with the cross and tomb of Jesus Christ. We are 'buried with him' (Romans 6:4). In baptism we are 'united with him in his death' (Romans 6:5).

Christian baptism as an act of burial expresses more than our repentance. It affirms the saving power of Christ's death on our behalf. As we go through this imitation of Christ's death, we declare that his death has life-transforming implications for our lives. Because Christ has died for us, we not only receive forgiveness for sin but we can be empowered by a new dynamic that has been released into human existence. Through the impact of Christ's death and resurrection upon our lives, it really is possible to experience radical change on the inside.

Paul develops this theme in several ways. Death, he reminds us, is a once-for-all experience. So Christ, having been raised from the dead, has conquered death once for all (Romans 6:9–10). His mastery over death is eternal, not temporary. Death has no claim upon him any more. Therefore, to be baptized into Christ's death means to lay hold of the hope of everlasting life. What Christ secured in the resurrection, he gladly shares with his followers. As we die into him in baptism, we receive anew the promise that death is merely a doorway through which we pass into the abundant life of heaven. This burial in baptism strengthens our resurrection hope. Because death has no mastery over Christ, it also has no mastery over those who are born again in Christ.

Paul also draws a parallel with the impact of death on marriage (Romans 7:1–6). However good or bad a particular marriage, death brings it to an end. Even so, Paul explains, when we enter into the death of Christ, we are released from the law. That means we are set free from any obligation to try to win God's favour on the treadmill of good works. New life in Christ is not for the deserving or outstanding. It's for everyone who knows that they don't deserve God's favour and have come to put their trust in the grace of the cross. The way to God is not by human effort but through the sacrifice of his own dear Son.

Every burial includes a death, and Paul argues that what dies is our slavery to sin. The sinful nature remains alive and well, fighting the cause of selfishness in our lives, but it no longer dominates us so easily. We can learn to resist our own selfish instincts with the supernatural resources of Christ. Burial into Christ is not a reason for mourning. This burial is a liberation, a dying into Christ that makes it possible for us to live as new creations. As Paul expressed this wonderful new beginning, 'the old has gone, the new has come' (2 Corinthians 5:17). Baptism as a kind of burial is an outward and visible sign of an inward and spiritual reality. The death of Christ is not simply something we look back to and depend upon. It's something we enter into. We die and are buried with Christ as we are united with him by faith, and this new connection with Christ can become very real in the experience of baptism.

What follows this burial into Christ is a daily choice. Paul invites us to count ourselves dead to sin but alive to God (Romans 6:11). He urges us to choose to offer ourselves to God, and not to sin, in our daily living (Romans 6:13). In other words, we are faced with new lifestyle decisions every day. Will I die to self, and live in the light of Christ's death and resurrection? Or will I live for self and ignore the significance of Christ's death and my submission to his lordship?

When I studied medieval poetry I came across an old Christian song with a memorable refrain: 'The grace of Christ is great enough.' Whatever our circumstances, however we may let God down, our heavenly Father is faithful to his promises and to the saving sacrifice of the cross. Some early Christians took this dying and rising principle so seriously they decided to save their baptism until as late in life as possible. They thought this was the best way to avoid the dangers of post-baptismal sin. Believing they had forgiveness and new life in Christ, they feared they could all too easily lose God's favour. Those Christians who kept putting off their baptism may have had good intentions, but they were also misguided. After baptism we don't return to life on the treadmill of works. There is no expiry date for divine grace, with the implication that we might have to fend for ourselves the other side of baptism. The saving mercy of the cross that applies to our lives before conversion continues to provide us with forgiveness and protection for the rest of our lives.

As we rise up out of the waters where we have been buried in baptism, we stand on the threshold of new opportunities.

In the light of our dying into Christ, we receive a continuing invitation to live a new life. And in the light of being united with Christ in his resurrection, we receive an unbreakable promise: one day we shall be united with our risen Saviour for all eternity.

It's a change of clothes

There's no suggestion that John the Baptist expected people to bring a change of clothes when they got baptized. Perhaps in the heat of Israel it was enough to take off your outer robe and stride out into the river. Or perhaps John's lifestyle was so simple that a change of clothes would have seemed like extravagant luxury. Although we are never given a practical checklist that tells us how the first Christians organized baptisms, Paul repeatedly uses a pair of phrases that indicate that a change of clothes quickly became a part of standard baptismal practice: 'take off' and 'put on'.

Pictures of getting dressed are used in the New Testament to describe three dimensions of Christian living. First, Paul compares believers with Roman soldiers going on guard duty (Romans 13:12–14; Ephesians 6:11–17). We live in the night-time of selfish living, and yet, Paul explains, we are the children of the day. Imagine soldiers going on duty without the protection of their armour. Such behaviour would be absurd. They would be putting themselves in immediate danger, and even putting their companions at risk. Therefore, just as we would never see soldiers on guard duty without their armour, we need to be protected in order to live well.

This picture speaks of life as a battle. As Christian soldiers we can experience life as a place of conflict, where we can be persecuted, mocked, teased or scorned for our faith. The wise and safe preparation to face temptation and opposition is to make sure we have been clothed in spiritual armour. Our heavenly Father has the power to keep us safe and to help us wage war according to the ways of Christ, in purity and firmness, patience and love. The fact that Paul instructs all believers to put on this armour makes it clear that God's protection is available for every Christian. This is not supernatural body armour reserved for God's generals alone. But nor is this protection automatic. We need to make a conscious and deliberate choice to follow Jesus day by day. Otherwise, we will be unprotected believers, putting ourselves in unnecessary spiritual and moral danger.

Some Christians have turned this instruction into a legalistic obligation. They pray through the spiritual armour of Ephesians 6 in a methodical, daily discipline. I don't want to knock that approach if it helps you, but I don't think the New Testament requires every believer to pray in such a literal way. The real issue is a conscious and continuing dependence on God for protection. When we go through life on automatic pilot, doing what comes naturally, we are bound to slip back into old habits of self-centred living.

The second picture of getting dressed looks forward to the resurrection. Paul assures his readers that the perishable will put on the imperishable (1 Corinthians 15:53–54). That is, when we leave behind our present, mortal body, we will be clothed with a resurrection body.

We have a pond in our back garden, and one of my most unpleasant tasks is to wash the filter. I put on my oldest, scruffiest clothes and wash everything thoroughly. As soon as I'm finished, it's time for a long, hot shower and some

clean, newly ironed clothes. The transformation is dramatic
and a great relief. It's wonderful to leave behind the last
traces of pond gunge. In a similar way, the resurrection
body will be so much better than our present bodies – no
matter how athletic or beautiful yours may be! Our new
bodies will suffer no sickness, struggle with no aches and
pains, face no prospect of death. Above all, our new bodies
will be exempt from any sinful nature, so our lives will be
pure and fulfilled. And that means our relationships will
always be constructive, taking delight in building one
another up and never slipping into misunderstanding or
gossip, malice or revenge.

The third picture concentrates on our daily moral choices
(Ephesians 4:22–24; Colossians 3:9–10, 12). First there is a
past event: Paul says we have already taken off the old self
and put on the new self. This is a way of describing repentance and conversion. But it also describes the experience of
baptism. We come to be baptized in one set of clothes, and
after immersion, having been buried into Christ and
cleansed in a spiritual bath, we get changed into new clothing which symbolizes a new start in life.

Second, Paul explains that Christians have all been taught
to take off their old way of life and to put on the new self.
This refers not only to teaching we have received before conversion and baptism, but also to our continuing discipleship
training. The first Christians understood clearly that their
task was not merely to bring people to confession of faith but
to establish them as living disciples. We need to help one
another to learn how to keep on growing in newness of life.

Third, there is a continuing experience of taking off and
putting on. Paul encourages believers to reject their old
instincts and put their selfish nature to a daily death. Weeds

spring up naturally in any garden. A gardener must be always diligent and regularly pull up the latest batch of invaders. Similarly, moral weeds infect Christian character, and need regular eviction. Paul lists many selfish instincts. It's unlikely that all will appear in equal measure in any particular Christian. Our efforts need to be concentrated on those for which our individual character provides fertile ground. But none of these moral weeds can be legitimately excused or explained away: 'sexual immorality, impurity, lust, evil desires and greed . . . anger, rage, malice, slander and filthy language . . .' (Colossians 3:5, 8).

As to the new self, Paul explains that while we have already put it on, it is being renewed within us on a continuing basis. When I was a young teenager, the custom was for parents to buy clothes at the start of the school year that their youngsters would 'grow into'. Some boys showed no visible sign of possessing hands until December, when fingers eventually managed to protrude from the end of their outsize blazer sleeves. Others grew so fast that by the end of the year there was a ten centimetre gap between the bottom of their trouser legs and the top of their shoes. In a similar way, having put on the new way of life by faith in Christ, it takes time to grow into it. Daily renewal, consciously and regularly putting off the old ways and putting on the new, means that we are living in the light of a crucial principle: growth in our character usually takes a long time. Of course there are some things that can be changed in an instant. But deep and lasting inner change cannot be rushed. We become more like Christ slowly, incrementally, sometimes painfully, step by step.

The fact that Paul has to tell Christians to continue to put off and put on underlines another important principle: living the new life is possible, but not automatic. It takes effort and deliberate choices to begin to change on the inside. If you leave a garden untended, the more vigorous plants overwhelm others, the weeds quickly colonize, and before long you have a jungle outside your back door. Without making these active decisions to put off and put on, without consciously checking and weeding our characters, we will soon revert to our old ways.

The experience of baptism is rich in itself but also sets a pattern for our daily lives. The change of clothes symbolizes a change on the inside that happens to us in conversion. From that moment we look forward to the ultimate change of clothes, when we shall at last receive our resurrection bodies. And once we have been baptized, we can look back to that experience to find inspiration for our daily choices, as we continue to take off the character of our old way of living and learn to grow into the 'clothing' of our new character in Christ.

One final thought before we move on from this picture of baptism as a change of clothing, which holds out the prospect of inner renewal in the transforming power of the love of Christ. Many churches have developed a custom of asking people to wear white clothes for their baptism. Some supply standard issue white robes; others suggest you wear white clothes of your own. I have several problems with these suggestions. First, I hate the idea of being baptized in an impersonal robe. God has made us in all the splendour of our individuality, and so it seems such a pity to depersonalize a moment as special as Christian baptism. Can you imagine the uproar if a church tried to make brides wear standard issue dresses instead of choosing their own!

Second, those robes are usually about as fashion

conscious as an anorak. If someone is a fashion slave, they need liberation, but our witness can only be hindered by dressing in drab uniformity. Surely we can leave such anti-fashion statements to the clone-like existence of China under the tyranny of Maoist Communism!

Third, and most important of all, the symbolism is all wrong. If a church really wants to encourage those being baptized to wear white, the best time to do so is not before baptism but after it. Otherwise we miss out on the New Testament symbolism of taking off and putting on.

We do not come to baptism as those who have earned the right, through our own exemplary behaviour. Rather, we come as sinners. If someone has not yet seen themselves to be a sinner, baptism is not for them. This is an event for sinners only, who have been saved by amazing grace. It is surely more fitting for us to come to baptism in our ordinary clothes, symbolizing our need of Christ. When we return from the changing rooms after baptism, the new clothes we have put on can then express our sense of celebration in whatever style and colours we happen to prefer, symbolizing the inner, spiritual reality that we really have been clothed with new life in Christ.

It's a sign of belonging

When our sons were about to start at their secondary school, we had to sign a parental contract. We committed ourselves to encouraging them to do their homework well and on time, to supporting the school's disciplinary standards, and to accepting the school's expectation that our sons would stay on into the sixth form. This was a kind of covenant, a commitment between the school and parents to work in partnership for the maximum advantage of the students. We had no trouble signing up, since these were values we were very happy to endorse.

The most familiar covenant for most people today is the marriage service. The emphasis has obviously shifted for many, so that the most important aspects often seem to be the wedding dress and the photographs, the reception and the honeymoon. Nonetheless, the central focus of the service is still the exchange of vows. A couple do not merely express their feelings towards one another; they make statements that express a free-will and binding dedication to one another, whatever joys or hardships their future life may bring. It's not 'I feel at the moment' but 'I will for life'. There are no get-out clauses in the wedding vows. It's not 'until I get bored of you', or 'until I find someone more interesting', but 'till death do us part'. A covenant commitment is about a wholehearted dedication to one another's best interests.

The Old Testament is built upon a series of covenants, in which God makes a commitment to his people and calls them to a commitment in response. After the Great Flood, God declared to Noah a covenant with all living creatures and for all generations (Genesis 9). Never again would the earth face total destruction by floods, and the enduring sign of this covenant is the rainbow. In this divine decree, God restrained himself from releasing upon the earth the judgement that men and women deserve for the enormity of our selfish living. This was a covenant of mercy and deferred judgement.

God declared to Abraham a new covenant (Genesis 15; 17). God promised Abraham, despite his childlessness, that he would become the father of many nations. In particular, God promised the land of Israel to the Jews and foretold the years of exile in Egypt. The sign of this covenant commitment was for every male descendant of Abraham to be circumcised. This was a covenant of provision and identity as God's covenant people.

Through Moses, God revealed in fullness his laws for good, safe and civilized living. The covenant was renewed at Sinai, and God emphasized the unique covenant status of the Jewish national identity as 'a kingdom of priests and a holy nation' (Exodus 19:6). This national covenant with God was reinforced in two ways: alongside the continuing practice of circumcising male children, the nation was called to public renewal of the covenant from time to time (for example Deuteronomy 29; Joshua 24). As this covenant was elaborated, it was seen to have a double significance. It was a covenant of sovereign grace: the Lord had chosen the Jews, revealing himself to them and rescuing them in their time of greatest crisis. But it was also a covenant of human responsibility. While God would not change his saving purposes, the impact of the covenant upon the Jews was double-sided: in obedience they would be blessed, but in moral and spiritual rebellion they would be cursed (Deuteronomy 28).

To David, God made a further covenant (2 Samuel 7). The first king of Israel had been disastrous, and so God had taken the kingdom from him and bestowed it upon David. Despite David's own failings, and there were many, God promised to make him great among the nations and give the Jews rest from their enemies throughout David's lifetime. Once again this was a covenant of divine mercy in which the Lord took the initiative on behalf of his undeserving servant. But this covenant is different from that with Moses. There is no balancing of curses with blessings. The Lord simply guarantees that David's house shall endure for ever.

For the Jews, this covenant became a mystery: when the Babylonians overthrew Jerusalem, the line of Davidic kings seemed to have come to an abrupt end. But the hope endured that one day God would raise up a king in the unbroken line of Davidic descent. The promised Messiah would be great David's greater son, whose kingdom would know no end. For Christians, therefore, this enduring covenant of grace that was originally made with King David finds its fulfilment in the coming of Christ. Jesus is the Servant King who rules over the kingdom of God, whose reign will endure for ever.

Jeremiah and Ezekiel both prophesied a new kind of divine initiative, designed to change the human heart. Jeremiah spoke of a 'new covenant' (Jeremiah 31:31–34). There would be two strands to God's new initiative: a once-for-all forgiveness, in which our offences would be blotted out beyond recall; and an inward moral and spiritual change, in which the law would somehow be inscribed upon our minds and hearts. Central to this new work of God would be an enduring covenant between God and his servants: 'I will be their God, and they will be my people' (Jeremiah 31:33).

These Old Testament covenants have several things in common. God takes the initiative in ways that are merciful and patient, opening up new opportunities for men and women. And God binds himself to us, committing himself to advantage his servants. In most of these covenants, God also calls us to a response of obedience and faith, for just as he dedicates himself to us, he calls us to dedicate ourselves to him. In other words, God's covenant blessings tend to come with strings attached. Not to exploit us, like the small print in an unreliable human contract. But with a call to practical service, since God knows best how human life can become the most rewarding, fulfilling and civilized. The more we live to God's glory and in obedience to his commands, the more we are able to enjoy the promised benefits of God's favour upon our lives.

The first Christians were Jews who were naturally soaked in all this covenantal thinking. God's commitment to them and their reciprocal commitment to God had been a part of their lives since infancy. And so Jesus was naturally seen to bring and make available God's ultimate covenant of salvation. Peter takes the language of the covenant with Israel at the time of Moses and applies it to the new international community of the church:

> But you are a chosen people, a royal priesthood, a holy nation, a people belonging to God, that you may declare the praises of him who called you out of darkness into his wonderful light. Once you were not a people, but now you are the people of God; once you had not received mercy, but now you have received mercy. (1 Peter 2:9–10)

The greatest covenant of all is found in Jesus Christ. This is God's supreme act of mercy, revealing himself and rescuing the lost through the self-sacrifice of the Son. What's more, this is a global covenant with no expiry date. Whatever our ethnic grouping, whatever our gender or generation, by faith in Christ we have been brought into covenant relationship with the living God and bound together with other believers as the covenant people of God.

This amazing enlargement and fulfilment of God's covenant promises to the Jews led to a very practical question. Since the Jews were circumcised to enter God's preliminary covenants, should Gentile Christians now share in this covenant ritual? Although some Jewish believers were very keen on that approach, the first Christians' official decision was a resounding NO! This was decided at a great gathering in Jerusalem, where James gave a profound and statesman-like conclusion to the great debate: 'It is my judgment, therefore, that we should not make it difficult for the Gentiles who are turning to God' (Acts 15:19).

The rite of entry to this new covenant in Christ was baptism. But note the crucial difference. The covenant with the Jews was national, and so every male child was circumcised. The adult response was to join in an expression of covenant renewal from time to time. Racial origin gave direct access to the rite of entry to the covenant. However, the new covenant, which is for all peoples, is entered not by race but by personal, saving faith. When the Spanish conquistadores arrived in South America, they thought they were serving Christ and advantaging the Indians by forcing them to be baptized at sword-point. This was a grotesque and barbaric misrepresentation of the Christian gospel. At the heart of Christianity is a personal, voluntary response of faith. True Christianity can never be imposed upon anyone.

The idea that adults can make promises on behalf of young children which the children are then obliged to keep in future years, was a concept acceptable in medieval Europe. But it leaves a sour taste in our mouths today. We live in a society that respects the autonomy of the individual. That's why we want to protect children from arranged marriages that are forced upon them by their parents, however well meaning the parental intentions may have been. In religion, as in politics and marriage, we are free to make up our own mind, in our own time and way. We can educate and inspire young children, but should never impose, pressurize or manipulate them: no one can ever be forced to become a truly believing Christian. The time for the covenant rite of baptism is when we are old enough to make our own response to the saving initiative of God's covenant of love.

In the wedding service, both parties are asked individually whether they choose to enter the marriage covenant. In a similar way, we can picture Christ as the bridegroom: 'Saviour, will you take this sinner.' His answer is ever the same: 'Always, yes.' And so we must consider our reply: 'Sinner, will you take this Jesus to be your Saviour?' No one else can make that decision for you. No one can force it upon you. But when we choose to say yes to Christ, we are assured of his yes to us.

When we are baptized, it is God's appointed sign of the new covenant, given to his followers by Christ himself. It is a sign of new belonging with God: we commit ourselves to the service of the One who has committed himself to us for all eternity. It is also a sign of new belonging among the people of God. We are saved individually, but called to live the Christian life together. And this belonging is universal. We belong not just in the family of our local church, but as a member of the worldwide church of Christ, irrespective of secondary matters like nationality and denomination. Your baptism declares this double belonging. It symbolizes a binding, two-way covenant of love with Father, Son and Holy Spirit, and an equally binding covenant of love with every believer who shares your living faith in Jesus Christ.

The meaning of baptism

We have seen in this chapter that the first Christians didn't just command and practise baptism, they explained and explored its meaning.

1. *It's a spiritual bath*, symbolizing that we are washed clean from every stain of sin.
2. *It's a burial*, showing our union with Christ in the power of his death and resurrection.
3. *It's a change of clothes*, establishing a break with the past and a new way of living, while also looking forward to our eventual clothing with the resurrection body.
4. *It's a sign of belonging*, in which we express our new covenant relationships – with Jesus Christ as our personal Saviour, and with the people of God as we seek to live in the love of Christ together.

Such wonderful truths can only find full expression in the baptism of believers. Without personal faith, this symbolic richness loses its meaning. But when we understand the deeper significance of this immersion, and enter into these saving truths with living faith, there is a wonderful sense of celebration built into the meaning of baptism. When we are immersed in water as believing Christians, we are able to enter fully into the great joy of this glorious gift of the risen Christ to his disciples. We are washed and buried, change our clothes and express a new belonging with God and his people.

Some people think of believers' baptism as little more than getting a good soaking if you happen to be keen on large quantities of water. The first Christians understood that true baptism can mean so much more. When we really understand and enter into the New Testament meaning of baptism, it can become one of the best and most memorable moments of our lives.

3

In the Name of God

In the name of the Father

The first time I took a camera with a zoom lens to my son's school sports day, I became a compulsive shutter-clicker. He was running in the 4×100, in the third leg, over the far side of the track. Before the race started, I was taking pictures of him. As the runners began the first and second legs, I continued to take pictures of him. When he was running, the film was flying through my camera. And after he had finished his part of the race – superbly, of course – I continued to take his picture as the runners of the last leg turned out of the bend and charged down the finishing straight. Suddenly I tried to hide my embarrassment as I realized that I had been so busy taking his picture I had forgotten to see which team actually won the race. In those moments of photographic frenzy I experienced a sudden and dramatic inner change. Without warning I had transformed instantaneously into Spike, the older bulldog in *Tom and Jerry* cartoons. My sense of pride and appreciation for my son welled up in a single phrase – 'That's my boy!'

Many Christians would not dream of picturing God's

attitude towards us in terms of a doting parent. Some think of God as a kind of police officer who has just caught some teenagers up to no good in the dark of the night. Others think of being summoned to a head teacher's office – not to be congratulated or for a pleasant conversation, but for instant and unavoidable reprimand. Deep in our hearts, many of us instinctively think that God is always marking the scorecard of our lives with phrases that have blighted many school reports. I'm not thinking of 'well done', 'good effort', or 'a pleasing term's work'. The phrases that sum up the attitude many people instinctively fear that God has towards us are 'Must try harder' and 'Could do better'.

The apostle Paul had a much more positive understanding of the Christian life. Before his conversion, Paul shared the slavish legalism of the Pharisees. They were so keen on pleasing God that they had become obsessive. Their initial good intentions degenerated disastrously. Jesus summed up the requirements of the Old Testament Law as loving God with our whole being and loving our neighbour as ourselves. For the Pharisees, rather than pleasing God with a lifestyle of love, they tried to avoid displeasing God through a lifestyle of legalism. In order to avoid breaking God's law, the Pharisees extended it, with countless extra rules and regulations that bound their lives. They became so trivial that their legalistic lifestyle was incomplete without counting the leaves on the herbs in their garden and giving a tenth to God. While I have never met a Christian who is a horticultural obsessive in this way, a Pharisaical climate of negativity has often infiltrated the church. The age of the Pharisees is not yet over – legalistic lifestyles still masquerade as true religion.

When Paul was converted, he made a complete break

with his past. The things in which he had once taken so much pride – his national and religious pedigree – he now counted as loss compared with the surpassing greatness of knowing Christ as Lord (Philippians 3:8). Paul's language is more robust than most modern translations – he describes his old ways as dung, manure. In recent years we have sometimes heard of new converts flushing illegal drugs down the toilet. The example of Paul suggests that it is not just illegal substances, but also our respectability, whether by birth or by personal effort, which needs to go down the pan. For as long as we hold tight to our own status and the merits of our achievements, we cannot enter fully into the abundance of God's saving grace. When we let go our own accomplishments, we can receive the fullness of salvation in Christ.

So what about after conversion? Is it best never to appreciate what we have done, in order to depend exclusively upon the cross of Christ? Paul regularly calls churches to live a life 'worthy' of the Lord and his followers (Romans 16:2; Ephesians 4:1; Philippians 1:27; Colossians 1:10; 1 Thessalonians 2:12). A worthy life is not a life that secures salvation through its own merits. A worthy life is one that spells out a huge THANK YOU to the crucified Saviour.

A life worthy of the Lord is a life that fulfils our potential in Christ. Most homes in the UK today are incomplete without a video recorder. The latest models come with a vast, sophisticated range of controls. With the capability to set different channels and times, they are designed for users to pre-programme a week's recordings. Recent research in Britain, however, suggests that most of us are pretty clueless about the more sophisticated controls. The only way most of us set our VCRs is by pressing the record button just before we go out. Our reasoning is simple: 'The programme I want to record comes on in an hour's time, so there should be plenty of tape left if I start recording now.' There is, however, a generation who are fully competent at VCR-programming, and their average age is ten. They don't read the manuals – they just keep pushing buttons until the machine does what they want. I have often thought that an electrical supplier could make a killing if it advertised VCRs that came with a free ten-year-old for the first week, to show us how to use it properly!

Our VCRs have sophisticated programming controls and one well-worn button, marked 'record'. We are buying capabilities that we never use. I often speak at conferences and celebrations where Christians tell me that there is a lot of potential in their church. I'd much rather hear this than be told that there is no potential at all. But there is a risk attached to these claims. The vital issue is not just having potential, but realizing it. I know that I don't want to have on my tombstone this kind of memorial:

He had a lot of potential.
Didn't do anything much with it.
But there was a lot of potential in there somewhere.

A life worthy of the Lord is a life that fulfils our potential in Christ. And no one ever fulfilled their Christian potential without active service, determination, focus and self-sacrifice. Once we have been saved, there's no time like the present to get up and get serving as a follower of Jesus Christ.

To the Colossians Paul adds a telling phrase to his familiar call to live a worthy life – that you may please God in every way (Colossians 1:10). Paul's confidence is unambiguous. Every Christian can please God – he really does want to be pleased with the way we live. And this pleasure can embrace every aspect of life. God's pleasure can rest upon our business dealings and our studies at school or college, our sporting achievements and the time we spend with our friends. The more we live by Christ's rule of love, the more we can know God's pleasure.

When Jesus was baptized, the Father declared his pleasure in his beloved Son: 'And a voice from heaven said, "This is my Son, whom I love; with him I am well pleased"' (Matthew 3:17). Likewise, when we are baptized as believers, the Father declares both his love for us and his pleasure in our obedience and faith. To be adopted as sons and daughters of God is to receive in full measure the loving favour the Father bestows equally and generously upon all his children. When you are baptized as a believer in Christ, the Father declares over your life, 'You have been adopted as my dear child, whom I love deeply.' The Father who loved the world so much that he sent his Son as Saviour, declares in the act of our baptism that his fatherly love rests upon us. To be baptized in the name of the Father is to declare our faith in a God of saving love.

Just as the Father takes pleasure in his eternal Son's baptism and life, so he can take pleasure in us. No one will take more pleasure than our Father in heaven as we fulfil our potential in Christ. When we are baptized as disciples of Jesus, most congregations will express their pleasure, maybe with smiles, with cheers or applause. Family, friends and everyone who is part of the local church will join in the celebration. But perhaps the greatest pleasure will be known by God the Father. Over our baptism the Father declares, 'With my beloved child, this day I am well pleased.'

To be baptized in the name of the Father is to take a

stand in his eternal love and pleasure. And that's just a beginning. The more you seek to fulfil your potential in Christ, the more the rest of your life will be marked by the loving pleasure of your Father in heaven. God wants to be well pleased with *you*!

In the name of the Son

The name of Jesus was absolutely central to the faith of the first Christians. Baptisms, prayers for healing and deliverance were all 'in the name of Jesus'. Peter declared emphatically that there is 'no other name under heaven' by which men and women may be saved (Acts 4:12). There was an exclusivity and a confidence in their preaching and praying. These convictions were not arrogant. The first Christians were not declaring their own merits, but only those of Christ. In his life, he never ceased to do just the right thing, whatever the circumstances. In his death, he showed remarkable dignity, dependence upon God, and willingness to forgive his murderers. In his resurrection, the Father vindicated him and demonstrated once for all the unique, saving authority that had been entrusted to Jesus.

For the writers of the New Testament, everything is centred upon Jesus. According to Mark's Gospel, Jesus' ministry continually provoked the same question: Who is this man? There was an unparalleled authority in his teaching, his healings and deliverance, and even in his response to the unruly forces of the natural world (Mark 1:22, 27; 4:41; 5:20). The most important decision we can take in life is what we make of Jesus.

Jesus is the supreme revelation of God. Throughout the history of the Jews God had revealed himself in two ways.

By his actions in Jewish history, supremely in their national liberation from slavery in Egypt, God demonstrated his mercy and power, first to his covenant people and through them to the entire human race. And in his words, both spoken and written, God revealed his priorities for men and women, calling for kindness and consistency in our personal lives, integrity and fairness in our business dealings, justice and compassion in our national policies. But in Jesus Christ, God went far beyond revelation by words and through dramatic historical interventions. God revealed himself in personal form. Jesus is the human face of God.

That's why the first Christians did not expend a lot of effort on developing philosophical arguments for the existence of God. The issue for them was not the theoretical possibility that some kind of God may exist. The first Christians saw no need to engage in endless philosophical debates, weighing the arguments on both sides. Instead they proclaimed the Son and invited people to discover in Jesus Christ just what God is really like. Jesus summed up this unique and supreme revelation of God: 'Anyone who has seen me has seen the Father' (John 14:9). In Jesus, therefore, we can discover the God who is personal and loving, patient and merciful, uncompromising in calling us to turn away from selfish living, and unyielding in his dedication to serving others with sacrificial, self-giving love. Our God has revealed himself directly, in the person of his Son.

Jesus is also the perfect model of true humanity. If we want to discover more about what it means to be fully human, Jesus shows us the way. We live in a world of gurus of the month: lifestyle experts whose moment in the spotlight is often followed by decades in obscurity. We have become increasingly addicted to image, fashion and first impressions. The cult of superficiality means that many TV, pop and movie idols are all surface and no depth. Not so Jesus. He had a joyous embrace of the good things in life, enjoying food, miraculously producing gallons of wine and clearly appreciating the beauty of the flora and fauna of Galilee. Seizing hold of life in all its richness, Jesus was a man who knew the pleasures of strong friendships and who was also comfortable with his own company, enjoying solitude as well as parties. He was in touch with his own physical and emotional needs, taking time out to rest rather than risk burn-out and freely acknowledging to the Father that he would rather not go through with his trial and crucifixion. Down to earth and real with himself and others, he managed always to make connections between the realities of every day and eternity. He not only believed in God, but was clearly in touch with the Father at all times.

Christians of all traditions have sometimes made heroes out of men and women whose religious practices, temperament and character are eccentric and imbalanced, intense and extreme when compared with Jesus. He is so much less religious and so much more down to earth than some of his acclaimed followers!

The first Christians not only proclaimed and worshipped Jesus, they wanted to follow him closely and express his life as best they could in the development of their own character and behaviour. Paul went so far as to say that he only wanted to allow himself two kinds of boast: the glory of Christ (1 Corinthians 1:31; 2 Corinthians 10:17; Galatians 6:14) and the weaknesses of Paul (2 Corinthians 11:30; 12:5, 9). That's why the early Christian leaders had no difficulty acknowledging their own limitations and failings. They had no need of image and style consultants. There were no spin doctors in the early church. Their confidence was not in their own giftedness, but in the absolute magnificence of the person of Jesus. Fashion magazines make ordinary people feel frumpy; diet magazines make normal people feel fat. If we want to know how best to live, we need to look instead at the character and priorities of Jesus Christ.

To be baptized in the name of Jesus not only represents public acceptance of the definitive revelation of his divinity and humanity. We also declare our absolute dependence upon him for the gift of salvation. In the New Testament there is no separating Jesus as Saviour from Jesus as Lord. There is never once a suggestion that we can become Christians by faith in the cross of Christ but delay until a later and more convenient moment our submission to his lordship. When we respond with faith to the person of Jesus, it's a case of all or nothing. Because he was crucified as God's appointed sacrifice of atonement, by faith we receive the forgiveness he has won for us. That means accepting him as Saviour. At the same time, because God raised him from the dead and he ascended to the place of authority in heaven, in order to accept him as Saviour we must also yield to him as Lord. We cannot chop Jesus into separate bits. To respond to Jesus with living faith is to yield to him simultaneously as both Saviour and Lord.

Of course we may fail to live up to this faithful obedience, which is why we continue to be dependent upon him for the free and enduring gift of salvation. But the early Christians were absolutely clear that salvation and submission went hand in hand as we respond to Jesus Christ, our Saviour and Lord. 'If you confess with your mouth, "Jesus is Lord," and believe in your heart that God raised him from the dead, you will be saved' (Romans 10:9).

In the name of the Spirit

The doctrine of the Trinity was not invented by theologians with brains the size of planets, in order to confuse the rest of us. The teaching was based upon early Christian experience, for God comes to us in three distinct ways. God gives himself to us as the Father, who has loved with everlasting love. God gives himself to us as the Son, who died in the place of God's enemies that we might receive eternal life. And God gives himself to us as the Holy Spirit, who pours God's love into our hearts, testifies to our spirit that we have become God's children and brings us the presence of Jesus in Jesus' absence. The one God gives of himself to us in three distinct persons. We acknowledge the mystery of the divine and the magnitude of the awesome love we have begun to encounter, when we describe God as one in three and three in one, in the everlasting community of self-giving love.

From time to time Christians have tended to lose sight of one person of the Trinity, or even to substitute something else in their place. The Father has almost disappeared from some Christians' thinking and experience – they focus almost entirely upon Jesus and the Spirit. Others have allowed the Spirit to be displaced by their devotion to anything from the Virgin Mary to the Bible itself. While the Bible has unique and supreme authority as God's word written, it always points beyond itself as a witness to the God who has revealed himself on its pages. The Bible should never be read merely as an end in itself. It is a collection of signposts towards Father, Son and Holy Spirit.

John the Baptist prepared the way for Jesus' command that we should be baptized in the name of the Holy Spirit alongside the Father and the Son. John emphasized that the baptism of repentance that he practised was no more than a preparation for the main event. John could immerse people in water, but he promised that the Greater One would baptize with the Holy Spirit.

So long as we choose the moment, rather than being pushed, immersion in water is a great experience. To jump or dive into cool water on a hot day is wonderfully refreshing. Greater still is the exhilaration of standing under the flow of a waterfall, the sun sparkling and glinting through the spray. Even so, to be immersed in water in our baptism – so long as we are confident that we won't be dropped – is a glorious experience of being united with Christ by faith, entering into the saving power of his death.

But John's words won't allow us to stop there. Like John, the church can baptize with water, but when our baptism is in the name of Jesus, the risen Christ makes freely available the promised gift of the Holy Spirit. To be immersed in water, drenched from head to foot and soaked in every part, is therefore a picture of how Jesus wants to supply us with the Holy Spirit. There is never any suggestion in the New Testament that the Holy Spirit is given in small and rationed portions. We are not given one teaspoon of Holy Spirit at our conversion, with a warning to be careful because that's all we're getting for life! The experience of water baptism is a picture of Jesus' best intentions towards every one of his followers. He wants to drench us in the Holy Spirit, soaking us in every part of our being.

This is no cause for alarm. When we are baptized by people we trust, we relax in their arms, knowing that they can be relied upon not only to push us under the water but also to bring us back to the surface. The New Testament plainly teaches that the Holy Spirit is sent from the Father and through the Son. No one could be more deserving of our trust than Jesus Christ. On every page of the Gospels, the way he dealt with individuals was precisely right for them. There was no pre-packaged, standardized, everyone-gets-the-same-treatment approach from our Saviour. He tailor made his response according to the needs and temperament of each individual. Therefore we can have absolute confidence in praying: 'Lord Jesus, even as these dear people immerse me in water, I invite you to immerse me in the Holy Spirit.'

There is much similarity in the New Testament between water and Spirit immersion. Both are for all Christians. Just as water baptism is the normal, standard, universal practice for new believers, there is never any suggestion that Spirit baptism is an optional extra for Christians who happen to like that sort of thing. The need to be filled and go on being filled with the Holy Spirit (Acts 1:8; Ephesians 5:18) was an integral part of discipleship for the first Christians.

Alongside these parallels is a profound and crucial contrast. Water baptism is once for all. No matter how much Christians may mess up after their baptism, we never read in the New Testament of any suggestion that they would be rebaptized after coming back to repentance and a new commitment. Baptism of believers was a one-off, symbolizing the glorious truth that the atoning sacrifice of Christ has been made once for all. The Christian who drifts into sin and then recovers their faith has no need to be baptized in water over again, because the power of salvation remains freely and fully available through the all-sufficient cross of Christ. Immersion in the Spirit, however, is a continuing and deepening opportunity for every believer. We all receive the Spirit at conversion, since only by the Spirit can we

confess that Jesus is Lord. But the fact that I have already
received the Spirit does not exempt me from praying to be
filled and filled again.

The evangelist D. L. Moody was once asked whether he
had been filled with the Spirit. 'Yes,' he replied, 'but I leak!'
We need to be filled again because sin and the cares of this
life distract us from openness to God. We need to be filled
again because when we give out to others, our spiritual
resources need to be topped up. We need to be filled again
because as the Spirit works in us he can increase our capa-
city to receive the Father's holy love. The once-in-a-lifetime
experience of immersion in water holds out the promise of
regular immersions in the Spirit of God. Christians who
neglect or avoid praying to be filled anew with the Holy
Spirit have taken leave of their spiritual birthright. When we
are not seeking to be filled with the Spirit we inevitably
experience a run-down in our spiritual effectiveness and
vitality.

Christians can so easily evade this opportunity. I was
converted in a church that was wary of the Holy Spirit.
As a result, I knew that I had received the Spirit at conversion, according to the Scriptures, but I was not at all
sure what to make of the third person of the Trinity. For
me, the breakthrough came in a communion service at the
church I attended as a student, when there was an opportunity to receive personal prayer at the end of communion. I was slowly brought to the conviction that I needed
actively and deliberately to ask for prayer to be filled with
the Spirit. I needed to ask, I needed to be filled, and I
needed to know that I had been filled. A friend of mine
compared my face before and after I received prayer that
evening. 'Before,' she said, 'you looked more miserable

than I had ever seen you. After, I had never seen you more radiant with joy!'

To be baptized in water in the name of the Holy Spirit is to open ourselves to the possibility of regular spiritual enrichment and recharging. God has promised to make himself continually available to us, if only we will ask submissively to be filled again with the Holy Spirit. So which is more important – water baptism or Spirit baptism? It's Spirit baptism, of course. When we baptize in water we are pointing towards a deeper spiritual reality made available to every believer in a continuing way. The risen Christ wants you not merely to be immersed once for all in water, but to be filled and go on being filled with the Holy Spirit.

Confession of faith

Faith comes first. To anyone familiar with the New Testament that should seem obvious. We are saved by faith in Christ Jesus, not by being religious, by acts of piety or any kind of good works. And thank God for that, because there are never enough good works in any life to put us right with God. When I first started thinking about baptism I rather carelessly talked about 'adult' baptism. But this is not what I now believe and practise. Merely being an adult is no qualification for baptism, any more than for salvation. The issue is not age, but faith. What we practise is not adult but believers' baptism.

There is no confusion in the New Testament. When Jesus gave the Great Commission he gave four clear commands (Matthew 28:18–20):

1. Go into all the world.

2. Make disciples of all nations.
3. Baptize them in the name of the Father, Son and Spirit.
4. Teach them to obey everything I have commanded you.

A disciple is a learner and a follower, just as the first disciples obeyed Jesus, left their nets and followed him. You can't consider yourself a wholehearted follower of Jesus until you come to faith. And Jesus made it plain that it is only after people have become new disciples that we should consider them eligible for baptism. Faith comes first.

We have to emphasize this simple and crucial truth over and over again. Faith really does need to come first. I think of one friend who grew up in a Christian home. His parents were both converted and he grew up learning about Jesus at home as well as at church. In his late teens, when some of his friends were preparing for baptism, Philip decided his time had come. He wanted to become a Christian. He really did want to receive forgiveness and new life through Jesus' death on the cross. And somehow he thought that getting baptized would do the trick. The Saturday night before his baptism the truth suddenly dawned: he was trusting his own act of being baptized, instead of trusting all that Jesus had already accomplished at the cross. Unless he came to saving faith, his baptism was worthless. Done without faith it could neither save him nor bring him to faith. Just in time for his baptism to be the real thing and not an act of empty conformity, Philip yielded his life to Christ.

Shortly after Jack became the new minister of a church, he preached on the vital need to be born again. Afterwards one of the deacons came up to him. This middle-aged man confessed to Jack that, although he was very religious and worked hard in that church, he had never personally come to faith. It was all theoretical and second-hand. Over the coming weeks, both this man and his wife came through to a radiant, saving faith in Christ. Then they were baptized. Now the unusual thing was that he had been baptized before as a teenager, at the same church and in the very same pool. It took courage for him to be baptized again. There was a risk of loss of face if anyone didn't understand. But that didn't really matter. He had discovered that most precious of gifts – a living relationship with Jesus Christ. There could be no better way to witness to the great change in his life than to demonstrate to the rest of the church the saving truth that faith must come first.

What about you? The decisive factor when considering baptism is not the quantity of water or the excitement of the occasion. The crucial issue is whether you have come to a personal, living faith. Please don't rely for ever on the faith of others. Please don't rely on the fact that you attend church regularly or that you have taken part in lots of church-based activities. No Christian leaders worth their salt will take it amiss if you need to explain that up till now your faith has all been rather second-hand. Jesus' words are very clear: if you want to become one of his true followers, you need to come to faith. And if you want to be baptized as he commanded, in the name of the Father, and of the Son and of the Holy Spirit, you must first make sure that you have this faith within you. Believers' baptism is a public confession that you have already come to saving faith in the Father, Son and Holy Spirit. Faith must come first.

4

Before and After Baptism

Many magazines contain articles and adverts that make
extravagant 'before and after' claims. From Dr Quack's miracle tonic for baldness, to 'ten easy steps to a new you', to the
latest scientific diet supplement, we are promised total life
transformation in an instant – or our money back. If only
real life were as simple, no woman would ever be overweight
and every man would have a complete head of hair and
bulging biceps. Baptism is no miracle cure. Selfish instincts
will continue to lurk within us and will struggle to resume
control of our lives. But baptism really does have a before
and after, and that's what we need to explore in this chapter.

Before: certain we are saved

A few people are converted out of the blue. They've never
previously given Jesus a second thought, never read the
Bible, never really talked with Christians. The first
encounter with real Christianity blows them away. Before
that moment in a million there had been no time for God.
All at once a new life has begun, with uncompromising
repentance and lasting faith.

For most of us, however, the journey towards faith is longer and slower. There are a number of issues that we work through gradually. We won't necessarily be methodical about it, perhaps feeling our way forward on several fronts at once. But a number of pieces need to fall into place before we are ready to begin a new life in Christ.

Does it work?

Before we listen to people's opinions, something needs to ring true about their lives. That's true of individuals. It's also true of churches. There has to be an added value seen in Christianity before we are willing to take it seriously. For me, as a young teenager, while some religious people seemed odd, bigoted, or no different from anyone else, there still seemed to be something indefinable but extra about the lives of at least some of the Christians I had met. They were ordinary people, but their faith was enriching their life experience and inspiring them to live more generously.

Does it make sense?

A faith that makes a positive difference is a faith worth looking into. Once we have begun to discern an indefinable 'something more' in some Christians, we are much more likely to attempt to discover just what and why Christians believe. For a faith to add up, it needs to pass two tests. It must make sense of life as we know it, demonstrating that its convictions are reasonable and rooted in the real world. It must also be self-consistent, providing a framework of teaching that comes together as a coherent whole.

Is it true?

Something can appear to make sense without being true. The medieval theory that the world was flat seemed to make good sense to most people. They could see horizons that looked like the outer limits of the earth. No one in Europe - except the ancient Vikings – knew that other peoples lived on the far side of the planet. The conviction was self-consistent, but not true. The fact that the Christian gospel does add up and makes sense of life provokes us to take the next step. It's one thing to say that Jesus gave some teaching 'with a lot of truth in it'. But the first Christians drew more radical conclusions because of the incomparibility of Jesus: his remarkable authority as a teacher and a healer and his untarnished moral integrity pointed towards his unique identity. And the empty tomb and the resurrection appearances pointed towards a unique and decisive event in history, with the potential to change the destiny of the human race. According to the first Christians, the only explanation that begins to make sense of Jesus, his claims, his person and his resurrection, is that he really was the Son of God in human form. If that really is true, then Christianity is not just about 'true insights' or something that 'may be true for you'. If Jesus really is the incarnate Son and the risen Saviour, then what he offers is universally and absolutely true, for every human being, in every generation and every culture.

Is it for me?

If Christianity is a revelation of absolute truth, then its message is for everyone. But a truth to which we commit must also be personal, addressing our own felt needs. We explore

Jesus' teaching to see whether it makes sense of our individual lives. We experiment with the Bible, worship and preaching, seeing whether God really does seem to speak into our personal needs and circumstances. We take our own temperature – emotional, intellectual and above all spiritual. We discover whether we are not just convinced but also attracted towards Christian teaching. Ultimately, it's not just a matter of rational conviction or an intuitive sense of belonging. We begin to develop a sense of the absolute necessity of the cross. The more we discover our individual need of a Saviour, the more readily we are drawn to a definite, personal conclusion: I needed Christ to die for me, otherwise I could not have been made right with God.

On the journey towards personal faith, we can therefore trace several stages of response:

I am slightly interested.

  I intend to find out more.

    I am intrigued.

      I am looking into it.

        It makes sense to me.

          I accept the essential Christian perspective on life.

          I'm convinced of the gospel.

          I'm compelled by my need of a Saviour.

          I have put my trust in Jesus.

I'm not for one moment suggesting that everyone makes a straight-line journey from atheism to saving faith. Some will hit conversion fast, like an express train reaching its final destination with no stops along the way. Many make progress that is more tentative and rambling. But however long it takes, every believer can eventually look back and see how the pieces have fallen into place.

Once we have been converted, we can continue to grow in our understanding and experience of the gospel truths that we have made our own. Knowing what we believe and why we believe are both crucial, but we also need to be sure that we really have become a Christian, and our feelings inevitably prove to be an unreliable guide. For some Christians, their new faith comes in like a high tide, sweeping them up to new emotional heights. For others, there is little immediate emotional impact. Some people's lives are like an emotional yo-yo and becoming a Christian makes no obvious difference to their ups and downs. It's vital to recognize that emotional responses are a by-product of living faith. They are never the main event. If we look for emotional highs as an end in themselves, we reduce faith in Christ to the spiritual equivalent of taking drugs. Much more profitable than leaning too hard upon our emotions is to discover a rock-solid foundation for our faith. We can identify seven pillars of assurance upon which we can build a secure faith, confident that we really have been born again and are fully accepted by God.

First, there is the pillar that we have prayed a prayer of commitment and really meant it. For some this is a titanic experience, so intense that the feelings are unforgettable. For others, the moment is less dramatic. When I was 16 I experienced six months or so in which I prayed a prayer of commitment at every opportunity. I believed in the truth of the gospel, but I was not yet sure whether I had made this faith my own. For those of us whose conversion did not take place instantaneously, it can really help to ink over an existing commitment by repeating a prayer of conversion once again. We can't be born again more than once, but the repetition can help us make sure that we've really broken through. There is a sample prayer of commitment on page 142, if that's something it would be helpful for you to repeat right now.

The second pillar of Christian security is the promises of the Bible. The more we read the Bible, the more we discover that it is jam-packed with glorious declarations of all that God guarantees to provide for his followers. Once we have made a personal commitment to Christ, all these promises belong to us. It's like having a cash card that gives us access to a millionaire's funds. Every promise of the Bible applies to us once we are in Christ. We can take promise after promise and apply it personally. For example:

- I am a new creation (2 Corinthians 5:17).
- I have eternal life in the Son (1 John 5:11–12).
- God will never leave nor forsake me (Hebrews 13:5).

The promises of the Bible are the bedrock of living faith. Feelings will come and go, and circumstances may change for better or worse. But God's promises are totally reliable and his word endures for ever.

The third pillar of assurance is evidence of inner change. Just like conversion itself, for some Christians inner change is sudden and dramatic. I have met believers whose lives have been changed in an instant. Drug abuse and other destructive habits have been snuffed out, never to return.

For others, change is a slower process, a journey into wholeness that can often feel like three steps forward and two steps back. Whatever our experience, it should still be possible to look back at our life since conversion and see clear evidence that God has been at work. There may be a long way to go, and we may wish that progress had been quicker in some areas, but as we look back and can trace at least some change in our behaviour and character, we take encouragement from this clear evidence that we really have been converted.

The fourth pillar of assurance is the witness of the Spirit. The New Testament teaches that the Spirit does not restrict himself to speaking through the supreme revelation of the Scriptures. He also speaks through preaching and prophecy, though never to contradict what has already been revealed in the Bible. But that is not all. The apostle Paul also spoke of the inner witness of the Spirit, testifying to our spirit that we really are God's beloved children (Romans 8: 16). Sometimes we rush around too fast to hear this inner testimony. Sometimes our lives are too noisy to make space to listen to God. But here is a deeper, intimate, inward revelation. Few things in life can be more inspiring and exciting than learning to tune in to this inner voice of the Holy Spirit. Into the depths of our innermost being he breathes the loving presence of our Father in heaven. The God who has adopted us as his beloved children will never abandon us, leaving us to make the most of life on our own. God gives us direct reassurance of his saving love in the inner testimony of the Holy Spirit.

The fifth pillar of assurance is the experience of belonging in God's family. Sooner or later some Christians are sure to drive us half crazy. Since all kinds of people become Christians, some who have been genuinely converted are likely to hold preferences and prejudices quite unlike our own. Some will confuse their personal tastes or the bias of their temperament with the gospel, and try to impose their ways upon us. Others slip into a negative mind-set, whether that is expressed in gossip and criticism or a sectarian mentality that quickly suspects that everyone else is practically guaranteed to be 'unsound'.

Despite the disappointments we are bound to experience in other professing Christians, we can also enjoy great privileges of love and care, support and appreciation. At its worst, church can be a foretaste of hell. At its best, it becomes a preview of heaven. There is huge encouragement from experiencing the family of God in action. Other believers can affirm our self-worth and build our confidence, not only in our abilities and value as a person, but also in the reality of our conversion. The more we are loved by our brothers and sisters in Christ, the more confident we can become that we have found our spiritual home in the family of God.

The sixth great pillar of assurance is the Lord's Supper. Like baptism, it was provided for his followers by Jesus and is an outstanding means of strengthening our faith. Every time we take communion we have a new opportunity to enjoy the meal of the undeserving. Our unworthiness comes face to face with the worthiness of Christ. In this simple meal we are nourished spiritually by the eternal impact of his saving death. As we eat and drink, the experience of the meal renews the promise to our minds, hearts and spirits that we really have become a disciple of Jesus Christ.

The seventh pillar of assurance is baptism. The event speaks gloriously of the power of the cross. After our baptism as a believer, for the rest of our lives we can look back with fond memories and declare: 'My baptism declared the glorious truth of Christ's power to save and my faith in him. I really do belong to Jesus, now and for all eternity!' The experience of baptism can make us stronger in the faith.

Before: getting ready

Once you are confident that you really have become a Christian, it's time to set a date for your baptism and you need to make preparations for the big day. Many churches offer special study groups for new Christians. Some will follow straight on from an evangelistic programme such as Alpha. Others will be tailor-made for those preparing for baptism. My own preference, following the pattern of the early church, is to encourage baptism of believers without undue delay, and then to provide a post-baptismal support group for the early days of discipleship. It's really helpful to be part of such a group, where we can ask our questions, work through our struggles, and learn from one another.

In addition to group preparation, it seems to me well worthwhile to have an opportunity for personal preparation for baptism. That means linking up with a more experienced Christian who can talk and pray with you from time to time. Maybe this will be a weekly Bible study for a month or two. Or maybe you will meet up once a month for a spiritual check-up to see how you are getting on. When I joined a gym I was allocated a personal trainer who was meant to check my progress every three months. In the same way, a one-to-one link with an established Christian may really help you on your way.

Before the great day of your baptism gets too close, you need to think about inviting your family and friends. As our lives get more and more busy, for most people a last-minute invitation will almost guarantee that they won't be able to come. It's important that they don't feel over-pressured. If they don't make your baptism but feel able to attend a later event, that's OK. If they feel so hassled about the invitation to your baptism that they resolve never to attend anything organized by your church, that's terrible! I think it's a good idea to invest in some printed invitation cards. The more you create an impression of an event that is very special and yet unthreatening, the more likely it is that your friends and family will be willing to make the effort to come along.

The night before your baptism is a good time for the final, practical preparations. Those who discover in the changing room that they have forgotten a towel or a change of shirt usually packed their bag two minutes before they dashed out of their home, already late for the service. My advice is to work through a simple checklist, get everything packed, and then go to sleep without any need for a mad dash the next day.

The night before is also a great time for spiritual preparation. It's good to spend an hour or so praying with some close friends, with others who are getting baptized, or with those who have prepared you for baptism. It's only natural to want to pray about your testimony, for your family and friends, for all that your baptism will mean to you, and that the celebration will be a great encouragement and inspiration for everyone present. Life has become so hectic that we can easily end up under-prepared for momentous events.

Don't stagger into your baptismal service, bleary-eyed, only half awake to the spiritual significance of the day. Make a conscious effort to get yourself ready – spiritually, mentally and emotionally. Like an athlete competing in an Olympic final, choose to experience your special moment to the full. Don't just go through the motions of being baptized. Make the most of it in every way!

After: facing pressures

After Jesus' baptism there came a ferocious spiritual back-lash. Like a football team that has just gone a goal down, or a boxer who has just taken a standing count, Satan was looking for a counter-punch. Satan hammered at Jesus in the desert, trying to undermine or destroy the positive impact of his baptism (Matthew 4:1–10).

In tempting Jesus, Satan appealed to three powerful human drives. *First, the desire for food.* After 40 days of fasting, Jesus must have been pretty hungry when Satan started talking about bread. The temptation was to think, 'I have an immediate need for food – never mind the consequences.'

Second, the attraction of making a spectacular impact without delay. Jesus' task was to declare the good news, and a death-defying leap from the heights of the Temple, from which, according to Satan, he would be kept safe by angelic intervention, seemed like a wonderful short-cut to being the centre of attention. The temptation was to think that the end would justify the means, but immoral short-cuts can never be justified before God.

Third, the desire for power. Jesus was the appointed King of the kingdom, and now Satan gave him the opportunity to rule the earth without having to walk the way of the cross. The rule of God made known in Jesus is expressed in self-giving love. The rule of Satan is self-centred love of power.

Behind these three attempts to probe human weaknesses were two searching insinuations. The first concerned Jesus' own identity, since Satan repeated a phrase of challenge: 'If you are the Son of God.' For Christians the equivalent attack on our identity is obvious: 'If you are really a committed Christian.' Similar attacks are likely to be faced at every stage of our lives, both upon our Christian identity and upon how well we are fulfilling our responsibilities as a son or daughter, a mother or father, a husband or wife, a church leader or member.

The second insinuation concerned the real meaning of the Bible. This is done through devious Scripture-twisting. This is typical of the great deceiver. If he tempted Christians with a direct invitation to become Satanists, most of us would have no hesitation in turning him down at once. What Satan likes to do is to distort the meaning of the Bible, so that it seems to justify our going with the flow of our selfish instincts. That's why, in the history of the church, there is always a grain of truth in heresy – it's what makes it attractive, and fools us into falling into line with false and destructive teaching. The intentions of Scripture-twisting are twofold: at the very least to undermine our confidence in what the Bible really says; at worst to cause us to sell out altogether to the twisted interpretation.

Throughout this onslaught, Jesus was protected by the Bible. He resisted temptation with his whole being, both mind and heart. Because he knew the Scriptures thoroughly and knew that thinking things through clearly is a crucial part of serving God well, Jesus was not going to be easily duped by the tempter. And because his heart was set on the things of God, he was going to stay focused, not distracted easily by the allure of forbidden fruit. As followers of Jesus we need to learn how to stay focused too. We also need to make the effort to get to know the Bible. One of the key reasons why today's Christians fall so easily into sin is our blatant ignorance of the Bible's teaching.

Satan tried to make the most of Jesus' time in the desert after his baptism. And he failed miserably. But we should not think of this period of temptation as a time when Satan took the initiative and God abandoned Jesus to the tempter's devices. Luke's Gospel spells out two crucial principles. Immediately after Jesus' baptism, he was 'full of the Holy Spirit' (Luke 4:1), which means he was anointed and equipped for the coming task. And it was the Holy Spirit who then decided to lead Jesus out into the desert (Luke 4:1), confident that he would overcome the evil one.

The time of temptation can also be seen as a time of strengthening. Temptations that are resisted strengthen our character and resolve. The strategy of the Spirit was not to cushion Jesus, keeping him away from all temptation, but to put him through a refiner's fire. In a similar way, the Holy Spirit does not want us to be weak-willed and wet, incapable of resisting temptation. The Spirit is looking for Christians with a bit of steel, a bit of edge. The kind of Christian who is incapable of living for Christ outside of Christian meetings is hardly worthy of the name Christian at all. Of course we all let God down sometimes, and forgiveness is freely available. Christ and his Spirit are willing to take on seemingly hopeless cases, which is how most of us feel about ourselves from time to time, and give us new opportunities to flourish as effective disciples. We need a determined resolve to get stuck in and make a real difference in this world with the good news of Jesus Christ.

There's no need to be fatalistic. Some Christians talk as if the desert experience is practically guaranteed as the direct result of getting baptized. It's as if you might as well book a double ticket in advance: immersion on Sunday, wilderness on Monday. The Bible never makes this connection universal or automatic. In my experience, some Christians have a tough time shortly after getting baptized, while others stay on a wonderful high for several weeks! There is definitely no reason to believe that there is no escape from the Monday morning wilderness feeling the day after you have been baptized.

Nonetheless, sooner or later we are sure to be tempted and put under pressure. That comes with the territory. If we are followers of Jesus, we will receive knocks from time to time that are intended to push us off course. However, we don't have to give in to every temptation and surrender to every pressure. We will fall into sin sometimes; that is sad and inescapable. But, as Paul put it, 'we are more than conquerors through him who loved us' (Romans 8:37). We are overcomers when we resist temptation with the help of the Spirit of Christ. And we are overcomers when we repent and receive forgiveness, justified freely through the power of the cross. In failure and success alike we depend on Christ, and in the power of his love we can overcome the evil one. Temptation is inevitable, but the triumph of the Son of God is totally assured. He has risen, so we can be confident that, whatever temptations and pressures we may face, forgiveness and restoration are freely and patiently available. Eventually we really will be able to overcome in the power of his saving love.

After: a pattern for life

Your baptism is a wonderful event to look forward to. It also provides a pattern for the rest of your Christian life.

We have seen that baptism is a spiritual bath in which our immersion symbolizes being washed clean. Whenever we come to God in confession and repentance we seek anew to be forgiven and cleansed from every stain of sin.

Baptism is a burial, which expresses our dying into Christ and the power of his death on the cross for us. Likewise, Jesus called us to take up our cross and follow him (Luke 9:23). There is an element of dying and rising in every day of active Christian discipleship as we choose to deny ourselves and follow after Jesus.

Baptism involves a change of clothes which symbolizes taking off the old life and putting on the new. As we choose to walk in newness of life, we continue to take off the old habits and values, growing into Jesus' alternative lifestyle of forgiveness and love. And we look forward to that ultimate 'change of clothes' when we finally receive our resurrection body and enter into everlasting life.

Baptism expresses a two-way covenant between us and the living God. We commit ourselves to a life of faith and service. At the same time, Father, Son and Holy Spirit bind themselves to us with cords of eternal love. In the thrilling experience of baptism and in our daily Christian walk, we continue to encounter the glorious triune God and his amazing covenant of love. We can keep on enjoying the extraordinary privileges of adoption by the Father, union with the Son and immersion in the Holy Spirit.

Enjoy the day of your baptism to the full, but don't let its significance fade over time into nothing more than a fond memory. Live out your baptism in your daily Christian living. The meaning and power of baptism can wonderfully enrich your Christian experience for the rest of your life on earth.

PART 2

Your Questions Answered

5

Time to Get Practical

What shall I say at my baptism?

The two things people say they fear most are death and speaking in public. In surveys, speaking in public usually comes out as the number one fear. That means many people would rather die than speak in front of an audience. Those whose weekly schedule is built around leading worship and preaching sometimes find this difficult to understand. Church leaders can take it for granted that anyone who wants to be baptized will be eager to give public testimony. But for some Christians this is a much more scary prospect than the baptism itself.

Everyone loves a story. And every single Christian has a unique story of how they came to faith and what difference it has made to their lives. Everyone present at your baptism, both believers and visitors, will be really interested in what you have to say. But this interest should not turn giving a testimony into the main event. I have known a few timid souls who were very keen to be baptized, but felt unable to go through with it all the time they thought that a verbal testimony was compulsory.

In the New Testament, I cannot think of a single instance of someone giving testimony at the time of their baptism. That surely means it cannot be made compulsory today. The New Testament instruction is simply and directly that we should be baptized as believers. So the first thing we need to do is to take away any unnecessary and inappropriate pressure. There's no need for every testimony to be a bells and whistles, all guns blazing, roller-coaster ride of verbal fireworks. In fact, you don't need to say anything at all. And if you do speak out, the important thing is to tell it like it is for you, rather than try to fit into, or even imitate, someone else's style of public speaking.

Just as some are worried about speaking at all, others are worried that their testimony is not dramatic enough. Some Christians get the impression that the only testimonies that really count describe sudden and dramatic life changes: 'I was a drug-taking gun-runner, but from the day of my conversion I began to establish a network of orphanages across the developing world.' If your story includes a dramatic conversion experience or a radical change of lifestyle, that's wonderful. But it's not compulsory. The reality is that, while all of us are sinners by nature, most of us have indulged only in the kinds of self-centredness that will never make the headlines.

According to surveys, the majority of Christians are unable to put a date on their conversion. About one-third can name the day. Two-thirds look back and see life in three stages: a time when they were definitely not believers by personal decision and living faith; an in-between time, when they were moving towards personal faith; and then a time of conscious personal commitment. This can often be the experience of those whose parents are Christian believers.

While some walk away from their parents' faith in teenage years and may then bounce back with a confident faith of their own, others make a steady transition from family practice to living faith, growing steadily into a definite, personal commitment.

Those who come to faith from outside the church can also experience a period of slow transition. My parents had me baptized as a baby, taught me the Lord's Prayer and sent me to Sunday school. As a teenager I decided to find out more about Christianity for myself, joining a youth group and reading the Bible and Christian books. There was a time when I was definitely not a believer. There was a time when I had definitely become a Christian. But in between there was a grey area, for about two years or so. I was growing in understanding and searching for the reality of God, without ever quite knowing whether I had actually made the transition and been born again. We all need to be born again, and know that we have been born again, but for some of us the period of spiritual labour and birth is very prolonged indeed.

What matters is not that your testimony is dramatic, nor that it fits a rigid pattern, nor that it is built around a definite conversion date. No, what really matters is that your testimony is real. This vital principle brings us to the third misunderstanding about testimonies. Some enthusiastic Christians assume that a testimony is only honouring to Christ if their lives since conversion have been trouble free and constantly filled with joy. Now if that has been your entire life experience, we should thank God for the special grace granted to you! Normal human experience includes many ups and downs. Circumstances are sometimes wonderfully easy, sometimes hard, distressing and confusing.

Emotions sometimes bathe our lives in a rosy glow of happiness and contentment, but at other times life becomes more gloomy, painful, confusing or sorrowful. For a few the experience of long-term depression means that shadows of bleakness are cast over almost every waking moment.

Many people look to religion for an escape from life's hardships. True Christianity is not about spiritual escapism, but rather about coping with whatever comes our way in life, in the company of Father, Son and Holy Spirit. Healing, answered prayer and wonderful joy are glorious Christian experiences. And so is strength in suffering, when we are sustained by God's love through the hardest of times. The Christian life really is a bed of roses, complete with thorns. The Father sometimes scatters discomforts into our lives to keep us hungry for heaven. The great climax of Jesus' life and ministry was his journey to the cross, and his emotional experience was twofold: he suffered in agony as he prayed to be spared from death (Matthew 26:36–46); and yet he went through with it, fulfilling the Father's best purposes, 'for the joy set before him' (Hebrews 12:2).

Those who follow Jesus in the way of the cross cannot reasonably expect an easy life, filled with nothing but joy. This was the foolish expectation of the Corinthians, and Paul had to remind them that there had been much suffering in his Christian experience. God's strength, according to Paul, is most apparent not in our human triumphs but in our weaknesses. God's love invades our every day, as the Holy Spirit inhabits ordinary, frail human lives. In our ups and downs, successes and failures, the reality of Christ's saving love is a witness to the world. The most moving Christian witness is often the person who has walked through very difficult circumstances, and yet has been so obviously kept by the power of God. What this means for your testimony is simple: only talk about a life filled with nothing but joy and peace if that's the way it really is. The gospel is about truth, not hype. And the reality of God at work in the ups and downs of your life is much more truthful and attractive than the myth of a problem-free existence. If you want people to listen to your testimony and be influenced by it, make sure that your words are real and stay real.

So far we have emphasized that a testimony is not compulsory, but can be very helpful. We have then seen that it needs to be a genuine account of your conversion and everyday Christian experience. In many churches, whether or not you give a personal testimony, you will be expected to answer some standard questions. The wording will vary from church to church, but the key issues are likely to be the same. Some churches may use the following questions to invite you to confirm that you have become a believer and that you want to live in surrender to Jesus as Lord:

- Do you confess that Jesus Christ is your Lord and Saviour, and you have put your trust in his death on the cross?
- Do you declare that you want to live as a disciple of Jesus Christ, day by day, in the power of the Holy Spirit?
- Do you confirm that baptism is your personal decision before Christ, made freely in response to his love?

This last question underlines the conviction that baptism should never be imposed upon anyone. Like conversion, true baptism is a voluntary, personal response of faith and obedience to the crucified and risen Saviour. To get baptized to please someone else, or because they have made you do

it, is an empty exercise, a worthless ritual of religious conformity. You are ready for true baptism when you have made
up your own mind, and want to get baptized in response to
the cross and the example and clear command of Jesus
Christ.

If you decide to give personal testimony at your baptism
– and I hope you will, because others will benefit enormously from hearing you – here are some practical steps to
help you prepare. There are three elements that are helpful
in any testimony: how you became a Christian; what difference it has made in your life; and thanks to God and to
those who have helped you. You may wish to include your
parents at the top of your list of people to thank. My parents have not been baptized as believers, but I know I owe
them an enormous debt of gratitude for all the ways in
which they have loved, taught, encouraged and supported
me over the years. If you can, affirm your natural family,
even as you experience the immersion that symbolizes your
entry into the eternal and spiritual family of God.

I recommend that you choose a special verse for your
baptism that sums up what Christ has come to mean to you.
I also encourage you to write out a draft of your testimony
word for word. This really helps in at least two ways. First,
the testimony can be checked in advance. Maybe it's too
long, and can be pruned to size. Maybe it's too rambling,
and the order needs sorting out. Maybe it's a bit confusing,
not quite putting into words what you really want to say. My
advice is that you try to get it written a week before your
baptism, so that there's time for someone else to read it
through and talk about it with you, and, if necessary, help
you knock it into shape.

A written testimony serves as a safety net. Maybe you will

choose to read it word for word. Maybe you will base your spoken words upon it. Either way, the written testimony can help keep you on track and reassure you that you are not on your own, making up the words from scratch. It's there as a back-up, even if you don't read it out at all. Just once I saw someone overcome by nerves during her testimony. She was a young mum, usually very confident and sunny, but as she gave her testimony and gave thanks to God for her husband and children, she began to weep and was obviously unable to continue speaking. Because her testimony had been written down, I was able to read for her the things she had really wanted to say about finding new life in Christ.

Timing is important. And that means we have to remember the KISS principle – Keep It Short, Stupid! It's always much better to stop with people wanting to hear more than to keep going when they are desperate for you to stop. Some talk for too long in their nervousness, losing all sense of time. Some experience an adrenaline rush at the warm response of a congregation and get carried away. These risks can be minimized in a couple of ways. If you write out and rehearse your testimony, you can make sure it fits in the appropriate time frame (I reckon three to five minutes is about right). In addition, I always think it's a wise precaution for the person leading the service to retain control of the microphone. It's not too difficult to prompt someone to hurry up when you are already standing next to them. It's much harder to reel them in if they have wandered across to the far side of the platform, taking the microphone with them.

There is another reason for standing next to the person giving testimony which is much more positive and reassuring. For many people this is likely to be one of their first experiences of public speaking and it can make you feel very vulnerable to stand on your own in front of a crowd of people, however well you may know some of them. I like to stand with those giving testimony, in order to give them a sense of reassurance and protection. I want them to know my wholehearted, personal support, and my availability should anything not quite go to plan during this very special moment in their lives.

What's best to wear?

Water has a dramatic impact on clothes. Some shrink and cling, displaying an accurate outline of the body underneath. Some become transparent, leaving nothing to the imagination. Others float. A skirt that has never previously been unruly is more than likely, when immersed in water, to rise up in a wide circumference around the legs of an unsuspecting wearer. In short, a poor choice of clothes can cause distraction, embarrassment, discomfort or even unintended sexual provocation!

Western churches have traditionally coped with these minor problems by providing 'baptismal gowns'. These are usually cavernous robes, minimum size 18, that look as if they had a past life as towelling marquees. Fashion dead and shapeless, they were heavily weighted around the hem to ensure not the slightest possibility of an upward drift when their wearer stepped into the water. If you still have some at your church, I recommend that they are offered to the Victoria and Albert Museum or put out for refuse collection as soon as possible.

In a previous chapter I explained why the symbolism of baptism as a change of clothes clearly suggests that the first

Christians would have tended not to choose to get baptized dressed all in white. Practical support for this advice is found in the fact that white clothes are particularly prone to becoming transparent when wet. What I strongly recommend is that you get baptized in your own clothes, wearing a swimsuit underneath in order to avoid accidental immodesty. Some people find that jeans become uncomfortably heavy when wet, so one obvious alternative to jeans and a t-shirt is a jogging suit. Our clothes express part of who we are, so it seems to me to be important to give people freedom of choice, as long as sensible precautions are taken.

Few years have been complete in my ministry without someone forgetting a change of clothing at a baptism. It seems obvious in the British climate that you will need a towel and a fresh set of clothes after being baptized. But some people are safe with nothing less than a written checklist, whether it is because they are nervous on the big day or just plain forgetful. Sometimes it's not the person being baptized but those doing the baptizing who come a cropper. One church leader called Peter only brought a change of clothes for his lower half, thinking his shirt would remain dry. The person he was baptizing was six feet tall and nearly as broad. As soon as the immersion took place, a tidal wave of monstrous proportions washed around the baptistry and Peter was soaked up to his armpits. A damp journey home in his car was hastily made, so that he could join in the party after the service in a reasonably dry condition.

If churches are to provide anything by way of clothing, it should be spare towels and emergency sets of spare clothes for the absent-minded and unprepared. At one church I served as minister, the changing facilities were non-existent and the toilets were woefully inadequate. If a church is aiming for sustained conversion growth and the budget will stretch, it's worth investing in changing rooms that come up to today's standards so that the facilities are doing nothing to put people off getting baptized.

For those being baptized, the requirements are simple:

- One set of clothes that won't cling, shrink, float or go transparent.
- A swimming costume to wear underneath.
- A complete change of clothes.
- A large towel.
- A hairbrush, hair-dryer etc., if required.
- A bag in which to carry home wet clothes.

Who does the baptizing?

In many churches the tradition has been that the minister or one of the elders does the baptizing. But the New Testament has some surprises for us. John's Gospel reports that for a while, early in his ministry, Jesus' followers were baptized. Many who had been followers of John the Baptist turned to Jesus, so that he was gaining and baptizing more disciples than John (John 3:26; 4:1). John then explains that Jesus did not actually baptize his new followers in person. He did the preaching and his disciples did the baptizing (4:2). Once Jesus realized the Pharisees had heard that he was becoming more successful than John, he decided to leave Judea and return to Galilee. The implication seems to be that the Pharisees would manipulate Jesus' success in calling people to baptism, so he deliberately took himself out of the limelight, returning to Galilee to continue his preaching ministry there.

The apostle Paul seems to have been inspired by Jesus' example, preferring to leave others to do the baptizing (1 Corinthians 1:14–17). Among the Corinthian converts, he could only remember baptizing Crispus, Gaius and the believers in Stephanas' household. Paul gave two reasons for his approach and neither reason had anything to do with a fear of water! First, his calling was to preach the gospel. He was not going to corner the market in ministries by claiming exclusively for himself important tasks that others in the local church were just as able to perform. Anyone who has ever baptized others will know what a privilege it is. Paul held himself back from a thoroughly enjoyable task because he was so concerned to equip and release Christians to exercise ministries for themselves. There is not the slightest hint in Paul of a priestly mentality that insists on reserving such privileges exclusively for those in full-time Christian leadership.

Second, Paul was desperately anxious to avoid any cult of personality. He was dedicated to the glory of Christ alone, but he was also realistic enough to recognize that some immature Christians would take a pride in the name of the person who baptized them. Paul shrank from every risk of creating a sub-group of Christians who might claim special rank as 'Paul's disciples' on the grounds that he had baptized them. He therefore concluded that it was better, as a rule, for him to avoid doing the baptizing himself.

When deacons and elders are mentioned in the New Testament, there is never once a suggestion that performing baptisms is part of their leadership job description. Baptizing is a ministry that belongs to the body of Christ. While there must have been some agreement as to who was suitable to do the baptizing, it was certainly not a task exclusively in the hands of any one individual or any particular team of leaders. The evidence suggests that whoever any particular local church considered suitable would have been allowed to take part in baptismal celebrations.

It may be that your local church has a set policy for who conducts baptisms. My own conviction is that the first Christians had a healthily relaxed attitude and the apostle Paul showed a refreshing caution about baptizing too many himself, rather than leaping into rivers every time an opportunity arose. In the churches I have led, I have developed a policy where everyone is baptized by two people. What I normally suggest is that one of those in the pool has some kind of leadership role in the church, while the other could be a close friend, a family member, or someone who has been particularly helpful to the person being baptized. There is a very practical reason for using two people. This method minimizes the possibility of anyone being dropped or proving too heavy to restore to an upright position. It also gives the maximum sense of security to anyone being baptized who is a bit nervous about deep water. Addressing these details helps everyone to concentrate on the baptism itself, dealing in advance with possible distractions as effectively as possible.

The most important reason for using two Christians to baptize each candidate is symbolic. This clearly demonstrates the truth that baptism is a ministry of the local church rather than something that should be monopolized by the ordained ministry. Like the apostle Paul, our great desire is for people to remember that they have been baptized into Christ, avoiding any misplaced emphasis upon being baptized by a particular Christian leader. If we accept Paul's example, we may find that the higher our profile becomes, the more cautious we are likely to be about performing the baptisms ourselves.

What's it like to be baptized?

For many Christians, their baptism will be the first time they have faced the congregation. Whether you come from a church of 20, 200 or 2,000, when everyone's eyes are upon you it's going to feel a much bigger crowd than when you are sitting with your friends. Some find this absolutely thrilling, reinforcing the excitement of the occasion. Others find it daunting, and need a moment to catch their breath.

That's why I like to do several things that help put people at their ease. I introduce the candidates to the congregation, so they don't have to do everything for themselves. I stand with them at the front, to give them a sense of protection and support. I ask them some pre-arranged questions of the kind mentioned earlier in this chapter, so that they can get into the swing of public speaking by saying something as simple as, 'Yes, I do.' And I explain that we'll now have some brief testimonies before getting to the actual baptisms. All these things help break the ice before we get to the main event. Of course, I don't have to do any of these things myself, but I do carry a responsibility to make sure that someone does them.

Regarding the water itself, make sure there is plenty of it. It's best to get in barefoot and carefully, to avoid slipping over. The temperature cannot be absolutely guaranteed, even with modern heating equipment. When I first joined one church, the heater resembled the element from a giant electric kettle. It looked ancient, may have been dangerous, and was hopelessly inefficient. It had to be stuck in the water for hours before making even the slightest difference. At one baptism in midwinter the fuse had blown early in the morning. When we arrived for the service, the heater was dead and the water was nearly frozen. Friends and family had been invited, so the baptism had to go ahead. We were baptizing a young married couple, and when the husband was immersed he shot back to the surface and almost leaped out of the water. He was the only person I have ever seen turn blue during his baptism. Judging by the smile on his face, the warmth of his inner joy had narrowly overcome the shock of the icy water.

More usually, people put a tentative toe in the water and have a pleasant surprise. With a good heater you are likely to be baptized in water that reminds you less of swimming in a mountain lake and more of soaking in a steaming bath. There's no point fighting the elements, shivering vigorously and feeling desperate to escape to the warmth of the changing rooms and a dry set of clothes. You really want to be able to relax and enjoy your baptism to the full.

It's impossible to generalize about the emotions that surround a big event. We are all different, we react in different ways, and sometimes we can even surprise ourselves. At weddings I have seen couples who grin so widely there is reason to fear that their jaws may be about to part company with the rest of their faces. Others begin to weep, and for some men this is so disconcerting that they carefully ensure they keep their back to the congregation so that their mates can't see. Still others look as if they are rehearsing for guard duty at Buckingham Palace, with not a flicker of emotion to be seen.

Most people experience baptism as a wonderfully joyful occasion. We may feel nervous at first, but our baptism is a fantastic celebration of the saving love of Christ. Each individual must be free to discover their own emotional responses. For some there is a great deal of weeping, as they are overcome by the undeserved love of their crucified Saviour. For others, this is a more solemn moment of covenant commitment, sealing their commitment to live as a follower of Christ. The most important advice I can give is don't go chasing any particular emotional experience. And never fall into the trap of seeking someone else's experience or judging them because their emotions are not an exact replica of your own. Seek Christ, and let your emotions find the level that is natural and personal for you as an individual in response to the wonder of God's saving love.

In the New Testament it is very common for people to receive prayer with the laying on of hands after being baptized. This is a great moment to pray for God's blessing and protection upon them, God's guidance for their future life and service, and for the Father and Son to fill them anew with the Holy Spirit. It is also a great moment to declare aloud any Bible verses or prophetic words that we feel God is giving them. I warmly commend prayer with the laying on of hands. It's not compulsory, but it's a great way of praying for God's blessing that goes right back to the first Christians. In my experience, it's best done in two stages. Immediately after baptism, while the newly baptized person is still standing in the pool, is a good time for someone to pray for them. It usually makes sense for this to be one of the people who have just performed the baptism.

I don't think that this is the best moment for prolonged prayer, for several reasons. After we have been soaked in water we tend to begin to shiver, even if the water has been pleasantly warm. When our clothes are soaked, it's difficult to concentrate for long on other people's prayers; we really need to get changed and comfortable first, especially if our clothes have become more clingy or transparent than we had expected. What's more, some people may respond as they are filled with the Spirit by swaying, rocking, trembling or falling to the ground. (Such responses should never be forced. If someone pushes those receiving prayer, they are not helping God but instead are producing a grievous distraction.)

My advice is not to rush into open-ended prayer while the newly baptized person stands shivering in the water. The best time for an extended opportunity for personal prayer ministry is after those who have been baptized have gone out, got changed and returned to the main meeting room. This allows the individual receiving prayer the opportunity to relax and concentrate upon God without any watery or shivery distractions. As to the laying on of hands, I like to invite a mixture of leaders and personal friends to come and lay on hands. In this way we represent the entire church as we pray together for God's mighty spiritual enrichment for those newly baptized.

When others pray for you, it's good to relax before Christ in an attitude of quiet surrender. Don't try too hard. Don't attempt to respond in any particular way. Don't talk, but concentrate on listening to the prayers and to the Holy Spirit. And resist any temptation to compare your response with that of anyone else. Receiving prayer, especially prayer to be filled anew with the Holy Spirit, is an opportunity to enter deep intimacy with Father, Son and Holy Spirit. God may come to us in assurance of his love, to bring conviction of sin, to renew a sense of calling, to bring new spiritual gifts, to remind us of a particular scripture, to manifest his glory, or in many other ways described and experienced in the Bible. The sooner we lay our agenda on one side, the sooner we will be in a position to receive every good gift that the Father has for us at this particular moment. When we know and trust the people who are praying for us, they won't feel distracting or threatening, and we can be relaxed and open in the presence of holy, heavenly love. Just as we relax in the arms of those who baptize us in water, trusting them to look after our best interests, we can surrender ourselves into the arms of the risen Christ, who pours out upon us the glorious gift of immersion in the Holy Spirit.

Who shall I invite?

The short answer is as many people as possible. Your baptism as a Christian believer is an unrepeatable moment of great joy and celebration. Just as you would want to invite friends and family to your wedding, invite them to your baptism. There is a note of caution to sound, and that is to make sure you don't put people under too much pressure. If they want to come, that's great. If they are reluctant, you can continue to witness to them on the slow-burn of daily life. There's no need to pressure people as if your total witnessing opportunity towards them is focused in this single event.

For some people your baptism will be a reason for rejoicing. They will be thrilled to attend. For others, the very notion of baptism by immersion will seem very unfamiliar, even weird. They may want to come along simply because they are intrigued to see something that sounds so unusual. The unfamiliarity that intrigues some will make others feel a little wary and uncomfortable. Do invite them, because you want everyone to know they will be very welcome. But if they express hesitation or make excuses, however unconvincing, be gracious in response. Better for them to feel free not to come than to feel pressured by you so much that they determine never to attend a Christian event for the rest of their lives.

After your baptism a party is a great idea, whether at the church premises, your home or even a hotel. You don't want such a wonderful celebration to have the feel of 'blink and you'll miss it'. Make the day as special as possible. If your budget will stretch, try to create something in between a birthday party and a wedding reception. You could cut a baptism cake and thank everyone for coming. You could even give some more of your testimony or get a friend to say what Jesus has come to mean to them or perform a song. Invite many. Enjoy much. Aim to make your day of celebration as perfect as possible.

6

Frequently Asked Questions

Readers will make use of this chapter in very different ways. Some will want to read everything in order to maximize their understanding. Others will want their particular question answered. For those in this category, the contents page lists all the questions so you can turn to each one quickly.

What if I'm too shy to give a testimony?

By far the most important thing is to be baptized as a believer. Most churches will probably want you at least to answer a couple of questions with a phrase such as 'Yes, I do'. But if the thought of speaking out is just too awful, I encourage you to explain your difficulty to a church leader. They should then be able to make suitable arrangements for you.

Keith was obviously ready to be baptized but was so shy that the thought of being at the front of church terrified him. I made a deal with him. 'Keith,' I said, 'I know and you know that you want to be baptized. So next time we have a baptism I would like you to bring a change of clothes. When we finish baptizing the others, I will catch your eye. If you give me a nod, we'll get you into the water without a moment's delay.' When Keith was eventually baptized, he was delighted with the whole experience, and couldn't understand why he had delayed for so long.

What if I cannot be immersed for health reasons?

Diane had severely limited vision and her eyesight was deteriorating rapidly. She avoided bright sunlight, and even in winter could only go outside wearing sunglasses and a visor. Her eyes were so sensitive that getting water in them would risk causing her great pain and might even speed her decline into blindness. Diane had become a Christian and really wanted to be baptized, but immersion was out of the question. Her first thought was that this disqualified her from baptism, and so for a long time she didn't even bother to mention her desire.

When we discovered that Diane wanted to be baptized, we quickly made special arrangements. She knelt by the baptistry and since it was too risky to get her face wet, we simply poured some water over her hands. She was thrilled, and so was everyone else. A very small quantity of water was used, but it was a wonderful baptism.

What if my parents disapprove?

The Bible instructs us to obey our parents in childhood and then to give them lifelong respect. The answer to this question partly depends on the age of the person faced with parental disapproval. If you are under 16, my advice is to wait until you are older. If you are 16 or older, I would encourage you to raise the issue with your parents and explain your thinking, being careful not to get into an argument if they react negatively.

Clara's parents were devout Anglicans. She was worried that her baptism as a believer might seem to them to be a rejection of her upbringing. She kept putting off the conversation, but eventually she felt she could wait no longer and had to talk it through with them. To her surprise, they were absolutely delighted. 'The most important thing to us is that you are living as a committed Christian,' they explained. 'If a different denominational setting is helpful to you, that's no problem to us at all.'

Charles' parents were more hostile. They needed reassurance that this was his settled decision, and not something forced upon him by some kind of cult. A visit from a couple of church leaders was enough to put them at their ease, and so we were able to go ahead with the baptism without any legacy of ill-feeling in the family.

For Amanda, the problem was not her parents, but her own insecurity. She had always been a very vulnerable person, having struggled with eating disorders for many years, and was deeply fearful of rejection by her parents. We therefore decided that it would be unwise to take forward the possibility of her being baptized until she was feeling much stronger in herself. Because of her particular personal needs, the most important thing for Amanda was not a quick baptism, but a long exposure to a loving and supportive fellowship.

Megan's father showed no flexibility at all. Stubbornness was probably a family trait. Megan was definite that she wanted to be baptized. Her father was just as definite that such behaviour was appalling. His denomination was the only true church, and he would certainly not attend his daughter's baptism. Megan was in her 20s, and more than old enough to know her own mind. She made the choice to be baptized despite her father's objections, convinced that she was obeying Christ by being baptized. Given the choice, she was determined to put Christ first. However, going against her father's wishes did not mean that she had to reject him, so she made a special effort to be gracious and loving, patient and appreciative towards her father. As an adult, she demonstrated her affection for her father not through unthinking and unconditional obedience, but by continued demonstrations of loving respect and appreciation, even when he didn't make it easy.

What if I was baptized as a baby?

There is not a single instance in the New Testament where anyone can prove that a baby was baptized. Every single person whose conversion is recorded in the New Testament is baptized as a believer, without exception. What's more, infant baptism can never carry the full symbolic weight attached to believers' baptism in the New Testament. Something that is imposed upon a baby, however good the intentions, cannot fully express any of the following: a confession of faith, a spiritual bath, a burial into Christ, a putting on of new life in Christ, an immersion in the Holy Spirit, full incorporation into God's family of believers.

There are two quite different ways of looking back on your infant baptism once you have become convinced that New Testament baptism is believers' baptism. Phil dismissed his infant baptism as a mistake, however well intended by his parents – a sacramental act without New Testament justification. He considered his believers' baptism to be his full and final compliance with the teaching of the New Testament. Shirley viewed her infant baptism more generously, as something well intended but insufficient in itself. She saw her believers' baptism as a fulfilment of her parents' aspirations. She considered her believers' baptism as a completion of what had begun when prayers were said for her as a baby. For Phil, the infant baptism was a mere human tradition, without real value. For Shirley, it was a prayerful preparation for the time when she eventually chose to be baptized as a believer.

Some who practise infant baptism complain that we practise rebaptism, but it is nothing of the sort. If someone went through believers' baptism a second time, that would rightly be called rebaptism, and should certainly be avoided. But when we baptize someone as a believer for the first time, we are clear that no previous encounter with water and prayer comes up to the mark. New Testament baptism is voluntary; christening is not. New Testament baptism follows on from a personal decision to follow Christ; christening is imposed upon children too young to make any faith choices for themselves. The choice to be baptized is yours!

You may choose to look back at your infant baptism and recognize its deficiencies – well-intended but insufficient. Or you may take a more robust view, rejecting it as a mistaken practice that emerged after the days of the New Testament and distorted New Testament Christianity. Either way, always try to be gracious to any who disagree. If you have become a Christian, and have become convinced that New Testament baptism is believers' baptism, it's time for you to be baptized.

What if I have been confirmed?

No one in the New Testament was confirmed. It was a later invention which attempts to cover some aspects of believers' baptism that are lost once you start baptizing infants. The candidates are invited to confirm their faith, and the presiding bishop prays for them to receive the Holy Spirit. The intention is to complete what has been begun in infant baptism.

Believers' baptism has a much more profound symbolic significance than confirmation. It carries the richness of New Testament practice and teaching. When I was confirmed as a teenager, it was a definite way of declaring my decision to become a Christian. But the practice is confusing. For some in my confirmation class, being confirmed was an expression of genuine, personal faith. For others, it was merely a religious rite of passage – something that was expected of young teenagers, with little or no significance in terms of Christian commitment and living faith. Of course a very similar kind of problem of a rite of passage devoid of saving grace is faced in believer-baptizing churches which fail to spell out that personal conversion, rather than reaching a certain age and attending a church youth group, is the decisive prerequisite for genuine believers' baptism.

In short, the fact that you have been confirmed is quite irrelevant, faced with believers' baptism. Whether we have been confirmed or not makes no difference: we are faced with exactly the same New Testament commands to be baptized as believers.

What if I was converted many years ago?

The first Christians were baptized without delay. It was a universal practice, and a standard part of Christian initiation. However, some Christians today are believers for many years before they face the issue of baptism. Some have never been baptized in any circumstances, according to the practice of any denomination. They may have never considered baptism, or they may have been waiting for a sense of personal conviction that the time was right. Others have been practising Christians for many years in an infant-baptizing church. They may have eventually been made to think about believers' baptism because they have moved church. Or maybe in reading the New Testament and Christian books they have become convinced that believers' baptism is the better way, in the light of New Testament teaching and practice.

Once they are convinced, some are ready for baptism immediately. Others are more hesitant. Since they have been believers for many years, they wonder whether they have missed the boat. Isn't it really too late in life for them to take part in an act of Christian initiation?

Ideally, according to New Testament practice, baptism should follow soon after conversion. But that doesn't mean that we forfeit the right to baptism once we have been converted for more than a certain number of months or years. After all, many of us were converted in churches that were very cautious about the Holy Spirit. But that didn't mean we were unable to discover in later years the need to go on being filled with the Spirit, together with receiving and using the widest possible range of spiritual gifts.

The two key arguments for those whose conversion was

many years ago are universality and obedience. The New Testament knows no exceptions to the practice of believers' baptism. Since every believer was baptized then, every believer should be now. Delay does not disqualify anyone. As to obedience, Jesus was baptized in order to 'fulfil all righteousness'. Likewise, we submit to the unambiguous command of Christ by being baptized. It also blesses others. When we are baptized, Christians are encouraged and non-Christians are pointed in the direction of living faith. However long the delay has been, and whatever the circumstances, now is a great time to go ahead and be baptized as a follower of Jesus Christ.

Is there a minimum age for baptism?

In Britain today, the age at which we move from childhood to adulthood is blurred. At 14 you can deliver newspapers and be paid for it. At 16 you can leave school, have sex, buy cigarettes and get married with your parents' permission. At 17 you can drive a car. At 18 you can vote, get married without parental permission, and buy alcoholic drinks. Rather than one definitive moment of entry to full adult responsibility, we experience a period of transition over a number of years.

Behind these restrictions is a desire to respect childhood. We would abandon our responsibility towards children if we gave them freedom to drive cars at any age. We protect children from adult exploitation by retaining a set age for sexual consent. It is obviously difficult to agree the age at which these protective measures no longer apply. That's why we have ended up with several different landmark birthdays at which we attain various elements of adult responsibility.

The age of entry to adult freedom and responsibility varies from country to country, but everyone agrees that there is an irreducible contrast between the two main stages of life: childhood dependence and adult independence.

The New Testament never suggests an age limit for believers' baptism. And yet the practice of baptism presupposes a significant level of personal responsibility. In order to be baptized as believers, we must be able to make vital and life-changing decisions for ourselves: to repent, to believe, to receive the Spirit, to follow Christ and to join his church. The New Testament preachers, writers and church leaders seem to have taken it for granted that people would have reached some measure of adult responsibility before they were ready for believers' baptism.

Young children can certainly come to living faith, but for many children, their own faith, however real, is caught up with their parents' faith. In early teenage years, with the onset of adolescence, this family experience of Christian faith will be tested. As we search to establish our own identity, we often experiment with discarding values and behaviour we have inherited from our parents. Only later do we reach a time when our sense of self is more settled and we know for sure that we have made Christian faith our own rather than being carried along by our parents' beliefs.

While young teenage years can be a testing time for childhood convictions, they are also a time of great peer pressure. Young people can become very dependent upon their circle of friends for approval and a sense of self-worth. As a result, they begin to copy one another, conforming to expectations imposed not by their parents but by the in-crowd. This can lead to outrageous clothing, fanatical support for the latest band to hit the charts, or experiments with illegal substances. It can also lead to all the members of a church youth group demanding baptism or confirmation simultaneously. These experiences of adolescent transitions suggest that it is wise to delay baptism until teenagers reach an age when they know they have made, with a reasonable degree of settled certainty, a definite and adult decision for themselves.

Since believers' baptism is once for all, I would much rather young people delay getting baptized than rush into a baptism they come to see later as premature and over-hasty. We saw earlier that people in Britain become eligible for marriage at two ages: 16 with parental consent, 18 without. In a similar way, I favour two ages of access to baptism: 14 with parental consent, 16 without. I would not suggest that these age limits are followed slavishly. There should be room for discretion according to particular circumstances. I have, however, found them useful guidelines, so long as one crucial principle is never forgotten. Reaching a certain age is never enough to qualify for believers' baptism, for there must always be evidence of a genuine, personal profession of faith.

Jesus gave two great acts of remembrance and encounter to his followers. Baptism is once for all. Communion can be repeated frequently (in fact it's a feast best celebrated often). Churches that practise infant baptism have traditionally said that you cannot take communion until you have been confirmed. But this seems to be the wrong order. In the New Testament the parallel between the Lord's Supper and the Jewish Passover meal is very strong. After all, it was the Passover that Jesus adapted in order to symbolize his imminent, sacrificial death. And since the Passover meal was held in family groups, the children were able to play a full part.

My own conclusion is that it makes good sense to extend

participation in communion to two groups of people. First, the young children of adult believers can share with them in the communion meal from time to time. I invite adults to decide for themselves whether to share some of their bread and wine with their children. Whatever their parents' decision, the children can also receive personal prayer for God's blessing and protection.

The second group of people to make an effort to include are young teenagers who profess faith but are still working through the identity struggles of early adolescence. To extend the Lord's Supper to them can be a great encouragement, demonstrating that we take them seriously and don't want them to feel excluded from the spiritual feast. When I first returned to church at the age of 15, I didn't feel ready for confirmation, but I know I would have been helped enormously by an invitation to take part in communion. In many denominations we rob our young teenagers of spiritual nourishment and the encouragement of a supportive and inclusive fellowship, by turning them into detached observers of the communion meal.

If a young teenager asks me about baptism and has clearly come to faith, this is the way I reply: 'I want to advise you not to rush into baptism. Let's pace ourselves towards baptism as a climax of your teenage years. But I want you to feel free to start taking communion with us right away. And let's see if there's some practical way in which you can use your gifts in the service of the church. We want to do everything we can to encourage you to grow strong in the faith.'

7

What About Young Children?

Jesus blessed children

New parents love to show off their children. New grandparents take much pleasure in debating which side of the
family contributed the nose or smile. For a few years at
least, children often become the centre of their parents' universe. It's hardly surprising that a group of parents decided
to ask Jesus to hold their children in his arms (Mark
10:13–16). They were looking for more than an affectionate
caress – they were seeking God's blessing.

The disciples reacted in their usual manner: wrongly.
Their intentions were to protect Jesus, and they tried to do
so by rebuking the parents. Presumably, in ruling out this
parental audience, they explained that Jesus was too busy or
too important to be bothered with young children. Immediately, Jesus rebuked his followers and made space for the
children. Throughout his ministry, he emphasized the value
of children and the lessons we can learn from them, especially about living faith.

In some churches children always seem to be an intru-
sion. They have to sit still, keep quiet and switch off, with

nothing to contribute and no moment in the service which makes much sense to them. The church has all too often slipped into the disciples' prejudice and assumed that God and true religion have no time for children. Jesus rejected out of hand the notion that God is only for grown-ups.

Throughout his ministry, Jesus affirmed children. He wanted little children welcomed in his name (Mark 9:37). He taught that we need to receive the good news like a child, with simplicity and trust (Mark 10:15). To be great in the kingdom of heaven we need to learn to become humble like little children (Matthew 18:4). Unlike those who wanted a style of religion that was for adults only, Jesus took delight in children's praise (Matthew 21:15–16).

Once his disciples had been put in their place and the children had been brought to him, Jesus took them in his arms, which gives some indication of the maximum age, or at least size, of the young children in this scene. Then he laid hands upon them and blessed them, just as their parents had requested. It is crucial to recognize that Jesus walked a middle path in expressing God's favour. He flatly refused to exclude the children, as if the kingdom of God were a child-free zone. And then he blessed them, *but he did not baptize them.* In the Gospels, as in Acts, baptism is reserved for those old enough to respond to the message that was preached – repent and believe. Jesus took great delight in affirming and blessing children, but during his ministry children were never baptized.

The baptism divide

At the time of the Reformation, the newly emerging Protestant churches had to decide what to do about baptism. The state church Protestants decided to retain the Roman Catholic practice of infant baptism. Four main arguments were offered: the tradition of the church, which had practised infant baptism for many centuries; the household baptisms of the New Testament; the covenant parallel between circumcision and infant baptism; and the symbolism of prevenient grace – that is, the grace of God which reaches out to us long before we respond in faith.

The independent Protestants rediscovered the practice of believers' baptism, and as a result experienced persecution by Roman Catholics and state church Protestants alike. The most extreme penalty they faced was death by drowning, based on the perverse notion that since they were so keen on water they might as well be treated to a lot more of it. In those days, therefore, to be baptized as a believer was extremely dangerous. You were only baptized if you were absolutely convinced that it was the right thing to do. These baptists rejected each of the state church arguments as fatally flawed: tradition has no authority when it contradicts the plain teaching of Scripture; there is no evidence that the household baptisms included young children; the parallel between circumcision and infant baptism is not found in the New Testament, but was developed later to justify a later and unbiblical church tradition; and the prevenient grace of God is expressed supremely and definitively at the cross of Christ rather than in a sacramental act unknown to the first Christians.

Far from pointing people towards saving faith, baptists saw infant baptism as profoundly misleading, whether in its Roman Catholic or state church Protestant form. Right across Europe, people assumed that they were Christian individuals who were living in Christian countries. They placed their hope not in personal, saving faith in Christ, but in the works righteousness of infant baptism: 'I was baptized as a baby in church, so I am obviously a Christian, by birth and by baptism.'

The circumcision debate

The first Christians were Jewish, and when Gentiles began to join the church, there was a great debate. Some Jewish believers said that the Gentiles should be circumcised and keep the Law of Moses. Others, including the apostle Paul, taught that all the Gentiles had to do was believe in Christ. He was convinced that far from helping Gentile Christians, the circumcision party were distracting them from the glorious gospel of salvation by the grace of God alone rather than by human effort.

This debate is a continuing undercurrent in the New Testament. It takes centre stage in Acts 15, when the Jerusalem Council agrees a policy on Gentile converts, and in Paul's letter to the Galatians, when Paul tackles the impact upon a young Gentile church of some visiting Jewish preachers who were insisting that circumcision was a requirement for every male convert. In Acts 15 the Judaizers speak first, and make their case succinctly: 'The Gentiles must be circumcised and required to obey the law of Moses' (Acts 15:5).

Peter, Paul and James all contribute to the debate that follows. They all develop the same theme, which Peter sums up in these words: 'We believe it is through the grace of our Lord Jesus that we are saved, just as they are' (Acts 15:11).

If the first Christians had practised infant baptism, they could have disposed of the case for circumcision with a simple argument. The Jews, they could have said, practise circumcision, but among us Christians it has been replaced by infant baptism. Game, set and match. The fact that this line of argument is never used, either in Acts or in the New Testament letters, can only lead us to one reasonable conclusion. The covenant parallel between circumcision and infant baptism was never mentioned in the New Testament because the first Christians did not develop such a parallel. The first Christians did not practise infant baptism and saw no need for a direct, sacramental replacement for circumcision.

The key contrast in Acts 15 is not between two outward acts, but rather between the outward act of circumcision and the inward response of saving faith. In a similar way, when Paul speaks of a new circumcision, he contrasts the Jewish practice – 'circumcision done by the hands of men' – with the inward transformation of Christians – 'the circumcision done by Christ'. This 'Christian circumcision', Paul explains, is the 'putting off of the sinful nature' (Colossians 2:11). The contrast is between the outward act of conformity in the Old Covenant and the inward reality of transformation which depends upon personal, saving faith in Christ. Baptism in the New Testament is not the new circumcision. When the first Christian believers were baptized, it was a public sign of an inward reality: they had already entered into the new, inward and spiritual relationship with Christ, by putting their trust in him as Saviour and Lord. Those who have been circumcised inwardly, by faith in Christ, are then eligible for the outward act of baptism as a believer.

When Paul wrote 1 Corinthians, there was a great deal of confusion at Corinth about mixed marriages where only one partner had been converted. Some wondered whether they should divorce their non-Christian partner. Paul said that they should stay with them unless the unbeliever took the initiative and demanded a divorce. Others were concerned about how God saw their children. Paul assured them that their children were 'holy' (1 Corinthians 7:14). Paul doesn't go into any detail, but he seems to be indicating that where one of the parents is a believer, their children are included within the covenant of love until such a time as they are able to make up their own minds about whether to live as a believing Christian.

The striking thing, once again, is the complete absence of any reference to infant baptism. If it had been the normal practice of the first Christians, Paul would surely have mentioned it in this debate. He could have said to the worried parent: 'You can be sure that God looks upon your children favourably, because the church was willing to baptize them.' The complete absence of any mention of infant baptism in the New Testament, especially in moments of great debate and controversy over circumcision and the status of children, can only lead to one logical conclusion. The first Christians never mentioned infant baptism because they never practised it. The only baptism they knew and encouraged was the baptism of believers.

Household baptisms

Defenders of infant baptism often refer to the occasions when we are told that a household was baptized. There are several household baptisms in the New Testament, including the following:

- Stephanas (1 Corinthians 1:16; 16:15);
- Cornelius (Acts 10–11);
- Lydia (Acts 16);
- the Philippian jailer (Acts 16);
- Crispus (Acts 18).

In three of these cases we are explicitly told that each member of the household was converted. Paul describes the household of Stephanas as 'the first converts in Achaia' (1 Corinthians 16:15). Baptism was not something imposed upon everyone else when Stephanas, the head of the household, became a Christian. They were all baptized because they were all converted. Similarly, we are told that Crispus and his entire household believed in the Lord. Luke reinforces the New Testament pattern by adding that many Corinthians subsequently became believers and were then baptized (Acts 18:8).

The baptism of Cornelius' household concluded a remarkable sequence of events. First he had been promised that Peter's message would make a wonderful impact: 'you and all your household will be saved' (Acts 11:14). Second, while Peter was still preaching, the household members were converted. Third, they were filled with the Spirit and began to speak in tongues and praise God. Fourth, Peter gave the instruction that they should be baptized with water, since God had already baptized them with the Holy Spirit. Baptism of the household followed on from conversion and Spirit baptism.

Two Philippian households were baptized: Lydia's and the jailer's. In Lydia's case we are told nothing about the other members of her household. The fact that she was a businesswoman makes it extremely likely, according to the customs of the day, that she was either single or widowed. She certainly offers hospitality to Paul and his team without any mention of a husband.

In the jailer's case, there is a violent earthquake around midnight which throws open the doors of the jail. Fearing that his prisoners must have escaped, the jailer is on the brink of killing himself when Paul calls out to reassure him that they have not run off. This leads to Paul preaching in the middle of the night to the jailer and 'to all the others in his house' (Acts 16:32). When Paul has finished, the jailer washes their wounds. And then the jailer and his family are baptized. There are spiritual and practical preconditions for these baptisms. In spiritual terms, the jailer's family must hear the gospel and respond in faith before water baptism becomes a relevant option. In practical terms, the family members are not only capable of hearing and believing for themselves, but do so in the middle of the night, and are awake enough to be baptized in the small hours.

We should be careful to recognize some important details in these incidents. First, we are not told even once that a young child was present in any of these households. To establish the practice of infant baptism on an argument from silence is very rocky ground indeed. Second, in every instance where we are given details about the household members, everyone who is baptized has already come to faith. Third, most if not all of these households would have contained servants. If every household member was baptized automatically when the head of the house was converted, then baptism would have been imposed not only upon any children who were present, but also upon every slave, irrespective of their age. Elderly relatives would presumably have been treated in the same way.

There are three fundamental problems with attempts to interpret household baptisms as a justification for infant baptism. First, it is an argument from silence, since we are never once told of young children being baptized in the New Testament. Second, if it proves anything, it proves too much, since if the first Christians did baptize the entire household automatically upon the conversion of the head of the house, not only young children but also slaves and elderly dependants would have had baptism thrust upon them, irrespective of their own religious convictions. What Luke reports, where there are several conversions in a home, is that every member of the household who comes to faith in Christ is then entitled to be baptized as a believer, and it is only natural for them to be baptized together. Third, such an interpretation flies in the face of the unambiguous teaching and practice of the New Testament Christians, since all the direct evidence we have points exclusively to the practice of believers' baptism. To build a case for infant baptism upon silence and speculation is to build upon sand. Infant baptism simply cannot be found in the pages of the New Testament. It is, in the view of believer-baptizing Christians, a lamentable misrepresentation of the biblical data. Only the familiarity of later church practice has made infant baptism seem plausible. The case just cannot be made from the New Testament. If infant baptism was practised and important among the first Christians, they would have told us so. As it is, the custom lacks biblical credibility. It is a classic instance of human tradition overriding the clear teaching and practice of the Bible. And the tragic result is generations of people who have been convinced that they are fully paid-up Christians, by birthright and infant baptism, without any need for personal, saving faith and a life of discipleship.

Including children

Christian adults have an awesome responsibility towards children. Jesus warned us in the gravest possible terms not to treat them badly. If we cause them to stumble, God's severe judgement is upon us (Matthew 18:6). Whatever our convictions about infant baptism, all Christians need to learn how to affirm and include children as part of today's church. We find it so easy to bore children out of the church, so we must make it an urgent priority to make church a boredom free zone and genuinely user friendly for children and teenagers.

This responsibility to protect children from stumbling rests on parents first, and then on the whole church. On Sunday mornings our children hear about love, forgiveness and faith. But do they hear a different story during Sunday lunch? Love can be usurped by gossip, forgiveness by criticism, and faith by cynicism and unbelief. Children can quickly learn that Jesus taught the positive way of love, but Christians often prefer the negative way of legalistic religion. We teach our children more by who we are than by what we say. Sadly, by the time they reach teenage years many children have become professional critics, well-schooled in the destructive art of finding fault with everyone.

Being around Jesus was immensely inspiring, but also hugely enjoyable for much of the time. The disciples may not have known what he was going to do next, but they were confident that he loved them and wanted the best for them. We need to cultivate that kind of experience for children, both at church and in the Christian home. Christian parents who are too busy to spend time with their children are just too busy. Buying them presents is no substitute for the best gifts of all: giving them your availability, support and love. Don't let your children down.

As to baptisms, I like to see children not just present but in the best seats, sitting around the baptistry for a close-up view. As they hear the testimonies, see the immersions and recognize the deep joy expressed by those being baptized, it helps them to grow into personal faith and prepare for the great day of celebration when they will be baptized. By avoiding infant baptism, we protect children so that they can enter into the full, New Testament privilege of believers' baptism at the right time in their lives.

Children cannot be made regenerate through prayers of thanksgiving and dedication. Nor can they be obliged to become Christians later as a result of promises that adults made on their behalf in their infancy. Salvation is by faith, not works. And every individual's free will must be respected at all times – true conversion simply cannot be imposed upon anyone.

What, then, is appropriate for babies? We give thanks to God for the gift of new life. We pray for God's blessing upon their lives and for God's protection in a world that can sometimes become difficult and dangerous. We pray for the parents, that they will grow into the astonishing responsibilities of parenthood. We also pray that the parents, supported by the church, will bring up their children in the knowledge of God and his ways. And we pray, above all, that the child will grow into a personal, saving faith, trusting in Jesus Christ as their Saviour and Lord. That's a wonderful and rich combination of prayers for any child. It's a great privilege to honour and bless children in such thoroughly biblical ways. We will not baptize children, but we will bless them gladly – just as Jesus did.

PART 3

If You're Still Unsure . . .

8

How to Become a Christian – a Second Chance at Life

Transplant miracle

One week before Easter 1997, Pete's doctor spoke words most people fear: 'You will have to think of your life in terms of months, not years.' It was terminal heart disease. By autumn 1997 Pete desperately needed a transplant. Given a beeper, he had to stay within reach of the hospital, and wait. Unable to sleep, he tried not to think too much about what he needed most – for Pete to stay alive, someone else would have to die.

Pete continued to deteriorate and collapsed several times. Eventually the transplant went ahead. The pain during recovery was torturous, but Pete was kept going by the joy of survival. Two years ago Pete had accepted death. Now he's learning to live again. No one knows how long he'll survive, but of one thing he is certain: he's been given a second chance at life.

Britain today

If ever a society needed a second chance, ours does. A *Panorama* journalist once adapted a phrase from

Shakespeare: 'Something's rotten in the state of Britain.' His theme was the appalling increase in violent crimes. In 1967 there were about 35,000 reported incidents; in 1977, well over 80,000; in 1987, 150,000. These figures are of course approximate. They may well be the tip of an iceberg. In October 1988 the Chief Constable of Sussex spelled out his fears: 'We are losing control of the streets.' The total amount of property stolen in Britain in 1992 was estimated to be worth £3 billion. The number of robberies reported each year has risen by 445 per cent between 1979 and 1996. According to Home Office statistics only 3 per cent of crimes in Britain in the 1990s result in a caution or conviction.

Sartre, the great novelist and philosopher, put it bluntly: 'Hell is other people' (*L'enfer, c'est les autres*). We have a foretaste of hell in the people who keep us off the streets or out of the city parks and woodlands after dark. The forces of hell seem to infect us, as seen in the increasing breakdown of marriages, relationships, family life and communities.

In easier times we looked at news coverage of the United States and said with complacent superiority, 'It could never happen here.' Now the once unthinkable is upon us. With ever more knives and guns on the streets, the violence of yesterday's America is the violence of Britain today. And the nightmare of ethnic cleansing in the Balkans shows that Europe can still be gripped by ancient racial animosities. It's difficult to disagree with Norman Mailer's damning conclusion: 'There's a beastliness in the marrow of the century.' Back in the seventeenth century, Thomas Hobbes considered life to be nasty, brutish and short; 300 years later, life is certainly a good deal longer, but the new waves of hi-tech violence are making life nasty and brutish once again.

Recently rock journalists got together to decide the best rock single of the last 40 years. Their number one? 'Satisfaction' by the Rolling Stones. Or, more accurately, 'I can't get no satisfaction'. The Stones' words still ring true today. Think of all the new creature comforts since Mick Jagger first belted out those lines. Colour TV (when it was first launched people worried about the dangerous new rays being emitted into their homes) and now digital TV, programmable washers, tumble driers, hi-fi systems, videos, microwaves, home computers, CDs, mini-discs, DVDs, satellite, cable and Internet, frequent holidays abroad, far more cars (every month London seems nearer to terminal congestion). Yet still we can't get real satisfaction. And now we must face the ever-increasing breakdown of society and relationships as well. What John Lennon sang remains true, both of us as individuals and of our society: the one thing we can't hide is when we're crippled inside. We are surely in crying need of a second chance at life.

In May 1988 a Harris/*Observer* poll asked how people saw themselves compared with ten years ago. Leaving aside pensioners and the unemployed, most said they were both richer and more free. So far so good. But most also acknowledged that they felt more selfish than ten years ago, and what's more, despite their material gains, more unhappy. In late 1998 *The Times* reported a continued and rapid growth in the sales of books on spirituality. Western Europeans are searching once again for a deeper fulfilment that cannot be found in the shopping malls. The same longing is being expressed right across the Western world: 'Beyond all our creature comforts, there must surely be more to life than this!'

Jesus' offer of a second chance

In Jesus' day there were many people dealing in superficial solutions to human selfishness. Some put everything down to diet. Eat the right things and everything will turn out fine. Others thought that complicated rituals of religious cleanliness would solve people's deepest problems. Maybe we can detect some similarities in today's preoccupations with additives, vitamins and antiseptic sprays.

Jesus presented a much more radical analysis of the human condition. He argued that it's not what comes into us from outside that's the root of our problems. Instead, he claimed, the moral equivalent of cancer lies deep within each one of us: 'For out of the heart come evil thoughts, murder, adultery, sexual immorality, theft, false testimony, slander. These are what make a man "unclean"; but eating with unwashed hands does not make him "unclean"' (Matthew 15:19–20).

Jesus' solution is as radical as his diagnosis. He offers no half measures. Jesus is nothing like a second-hand car salesman, who means by a second chance a new lick of paint over old rust. A second chance means not just a change of diet or a new code of conduct, but rather an inner transformation. Jesus presents us with an opportunity for inner change in three dimensions.

1. Forgiveness

All of us need to be forgiven. We often don't manage to live up to our own standards. We certainly don't live up to God's values, which are revealed in the Bible and demonstrated in the life of Jesus. In the Bible this living for self is called 'sin'. The Bible explains that our sin gets between us and God like a barrier. This is true, not just for big time gangsters or murderers, but for every human being. We are cut off from God by our own wrongdoing, and unable to make amends through our own efforts.

2. Power for living

Maybe your parents had a cooker that was converted for use with North Sea gas. That conversion would have done no good at all unless the cooker was connected to a new gas supply. In the same way, Jesus promised not to leave us to our own resources once we receive forgiveness. Instead, he sends the Holy Spirit, the life and presence of God himself, to provide new power for living. We can begin over again, knowing that the Spirit of Jesus has now taken up residence within us, making a new way of life really possible.

3. Knowing God personally

Jesus promised to bring us into a new relationship with God. He said we could know the Creator of the universe personally. He even promised that we could dare to call him Father. Ever since, Christians have experienced the wonder of God's personal love flowing into their lives. Men and women simply cannot find lasting satisfaction until they discover and experience God's personal love. Augustine put it like this: 'The human spirit remains restless until it finds its rest in God.'

What was true of Pete's heart transplant is true for Jesus' offer of a second chance. Someone else has to die to make it possible. Jesus is the only person ever to have lived without committing any sin at all. So when Jesus died, he was able to bear your sin and mine. Because Jesus died in our place, we can be forgiven and set free from every stain of sin. What's more, we can receive a transplant of Jesus' perfect standing before God the Father. When Jesus offers a second chance, it's a second chance at abundant life. A second chance at depth. A second chance that can really work and that lasts for ever.

No half measures

Have you ever modernized a kitchen? We had to in the first home we bought, down in Tonbridge, Kent. We were up to our eyes in mortgage, so we couldn't afford to employ builders. Each night, as soon as we were home from work, we'd get onto the next stage – a power drill in one hand and the *Readers' Digest DIY Manual* in the other. During the many, many weeks of vital preparation, friends would sometimes call round and say with their eyes, if not with their voices, 'Is that all you've done?' At long last we got onto the decorating, and only then did we really seem to receive much appreciation. It's only the finishing touches that most people ever notice.

A few years later we moved to a house where a brand new kitchen had recently been fitted. We went away for a holiday, and when we came back there was an unexpected problem. The paper wrappings on tins in one cupboard had gone mouldy. In came the professionals and when they tested the walls the needle swung off the end of the scale on their meter. There was not so much a dampness as a wetness problem. Out went the kitchen units, then the plaster, and then the concrete floor. The entire room was gutted. For as long as the damp was there, the problem could only get worse. Though it had concealed the damp, the modernized finish was totally incapable of dealing with the underlying problem.

Only Jesus can offer you this second chance at life, and he's never superficial. He certainly doesn't offer merely to tart up the surface of your life. A second chance means deep inward change. A second chance means a life transplant, right at the centre of our being. A second chance is God's gift, which he offers you this very moment, in Christ Jesus.

It doesn't matter who you are. It doesn't matter what you've done. It doesn't matter what status or lack of status you have in society or in the church. I heard recently of an evangelist who walked up to a man in the congregation one night. The man had a heavy frown on his face and looked as if someone had forcibly stuffed half a dozen prunes into his mouth. The evangelist put a hand on the man's shoulder and asked if he wanted to become a Christian. The man growled back at the evangelist, 'I'll have you know I'm a deacon in this church!' Without a moment's hesitation the evangelist replied, 'Well, don't let that get in your way!'

Receiving from Jesus

Jesus really is offering you a second chance. If you take it, he has promised never to turn you away. If you reject it, then one day there'll be no time left for second chances. At the last judgement, Jesus won't press his eternal presence upon those who have already rejected him. Do you want this second chance at life? Are you ready to receive everything that Jesus offers? Then you need to take these three steps.

1. You need to confess and turn away from selfish living

You need to tell God that you need forgiveness, because you have failed to live by God's standards. None of us has loved

God with all our strength, or loved our neighbour as much as we love ourselves.

2. *You need to believe*

You need to thank God that Jesus' promises are true and that when he died on the cross, he died for you.

3. *You need to ask*

Invite Jesus to come into your life and give you a second chance.

If you are ready for the second chance that Jesus offers, you can make this prayer your own:

> Lord Jesus Christ,
> I'm sorry that you had to die on the cross for me,
> but I'm glad that you did.
> I need to receive your forgiveness,
> and want to begin a new life in the power of your love.
> Please come into my life:
>   as my Saviour to forgive me,
>   as my Lord to rule over me,
>   and as my Friend, to love me and be with me for ever.
> Thank you that, now I give my life to you,
> I am yours for ever
> and you have promised never to forget me or let me go.
> Amen.

It's important to tell other Christians as soon as possible about your decision to pray this prayer. They will be thrilled for you and will want to do all they can to help you grow strong in your new life in Christ and enjoy being a Christian to the full. Remember, whenever anyone puts their trust in Christ, they receive the most wonderful gift: *a second chance at life*.

9

Is Anyone Thirsty? Receiving More of the Holy Spirit

If you look out of a British bedroom window first thing in the morning and see that it's raining outside, two reactions are unlikely: spontaneous thankfulness to God (unless you happen to be a particularly keen gardener living under a hosepipe ban!) and surprise. We don't get more rain in Britain than they do in the rest of Northern Europe. It just seems to arrive in a different sort of way. In many countries there are plenty of days without any rain at all and some days when it buckets down relentlessly. In Britain, there are simply lots of days when it rains a bit. Of all the peoples of the world, the British are likely to find it particularly difficult to comprehend the festival at which the Jews gave thanks for the rain. The chief purpose of rain in our country is to give us something to complain about rather than something for which to give thanks to God!

The Middle Eastern experience of rain is quite different. There are two rainy seasons – the autumn and spring rains – with long, hot, reliably dry periods in the intervening months. Long ago, the Jews developed a profound sense of dependence on God to supply the rains in season. Growing out of that physical reliance upon the rains, the Jewish prophets and poets developed an imagery to express their deeper spiritual longings: the coming of the Spirit was promised like rain on dry ground and streams in the desert.

A few years ago I was in Israel when the spring rains were due. The morning I woke up to the sound of rain I was absolutely delighted. I drove out around the hills of Galilee under a deluge. Passing through Nazareth, the streets were awash, the drains overwhelmed by the huge amounts of water suddenly drenching the town. My first impression was the sheer volume of rain. My second was how quickly it was absorbed into the parched ground, without any obvious impact.

The next day I saw a warning for tourists. In the dry season, many visitors to Israel like to go on a pilgrimage in the desert, usually identifying with Jesus when he was tempted in the wilderness, or with Moses' generation who left Egyptian slavery behind on their long march to freedom. To avoid getting lost, many tourists follow the course of dry river beds, no doubt congratulating themselves on their resourcefulness. The warning was for these happy wanderers, advising them, now that the rains had come, to avoid walking these dry river beds. Hidden from view, the water table was rising. Suddenly the water would burst out from the ground, and in an instant the streams and rivers would be restored to full flood. The raging torrent would sweep all before it, clearing away the carcasses of any animals that had wandered into the desert, any plants that had died, and, of course, any unsuspecting tourists. That gave me my third insight into the Old Testament prophecies of God sending his Spirit like the autumn and spring rains. The heavy rains produce a torrent that sweeps all before it and cleanses the land.

A few days later we drove down to Jerusalem. Our map said we were driving through desert regions. But our eyes saw a quite different kind of view. The hillsides were richly carpeted with flowers in full bloom. Plants don't have time to spare in a harsh climate. In Britain the growing season is long and leisurely. There's no need to hurry through the life cycle. In the near desert conditions of Israel, moisture is unlikely to be around for long. Once the rains hit the seeds, it's a race against time. The entire growing season must be compressed into a narrow window of opportunity before the relentless sunshine burns everything dry as dust once again.

I had already seen the great deluge, the apparent disappearance of the rain into parched ground, and the cleansing torrent. These experiences greatly enriched my understanding of the Old Testament promises that God would send his Spirit like the spring and autumn rains. But now I saw the fourth great impact. It's like an experience of accelerated time. Suddenly the hills are filled with an abundant beauty and fruitfulness: when the rains come, the world of nature really comes alive, bursting into growth, flower and fruit.

These biblical promises and life experiences shaped the Feast of the Tabernacles, which was the Jewish festival of thanksgiving for the rain. Each year the Jews would give thanks for the rains of the past year and pray that God would send rain in season during the coming year. The Feast acknowledged their dependence upon God for farming success and for food on the table. At the same time, the Feast looked beyond material provision to the spiritual promises of the prophets – that God would send his Spirit like the spring and autumn rains. Above all, the Feast looked back to Ezekiel's vision of a new river that would start in Jerusalem and bring life wherever it flowed (Ezekiel 47:9).

Each year, at the climax of the Feast, a special container would be taken from the Temple and filled with water. Back in the Temple precincts, the water would be poured out upon the ground. It was an enacted prayer, in which the Jews presented their heartfelt longing. Even as they were able to pour out physical water upon the ground, their great desire was that God would be gracious to fulfil his promise and pour out his Spirit upon their thirsty lives.

John's Gospel tells us that one year when Jesus was visiting Jerusalem, he kept a low profile until the last and greatest day of this Feast. Then he stood up and spoke out in a loud voice: 'If anyone is thirsty, let him come to me and drink. Whoever believes in me, as the Scripture has said, streams of living water will flow from within them' (John 7:37–38).

This way of talking was typical of Jesus. For the Jews, the implications were startling. In line with their long-established desire for God to send the promised rain of his Spirit, Jesus is declaring, 'The river of God starts with me.' This is one of Jesus' oblique claims to divinity: in his person the promise of God is fulfilled. What God had said he would do one day is now accomplished through Jesus' ministry.

After this astonishing declaration, John tells us what happened next. Absolutely nothing. John then explains that while Jesus really did come to set God's river flowing, first he had to be 'glorified' and only then could the promise of the Spirit be fulfilled. 'Glorified' is used in a special way in

John's Gospel. Normally it would mean a demonstration of majesty, might and splendour. But John's Gospel uses 'glorify' to speak of the cross.

Nothing could have been further from the thinking of the Roman Empire. Crucifixion was designed to be a slow, wretched, painful and humiliating way to die. It was meant to send out an uncompromising message: 'Don't mess with Rome.' As for the Jews, the Old Testament said that anyone who died hanging on a tree was under God's curse, so death on a cross would be taken to mean quite the reverse of glorification. For the principalities and powers, this death looked like the ultimate defeat of the Son of God, spurned by those he had come to serve with his message of love and forgiveness. Paul spells out the reversal of this demonic first impression of Christ's crucifixion, explaining that Christ made a public spectacle of the powers, stripping them of their presumed authority and triumphing over them by the power of the cross (Colossians 2:15). The glory of God, which is wonderfully apparent in the splendour of creation and the majesty of heaven, finds its fullest expression in the cross of Christ. When Christ gives up his life for the sake of his enemies, the extravagant mercy of God is made manifest in all its glory.

A few years ago the newspaper headlines were filled with stories of elephant idols in Hindu temples that were drinking milk. Crowds of Hindus queued up to serve milk to these statues. There were several theories to explain this curiosity. Some suggested it was a simple physical reaction – the statues were made of porous rock that would naturally absorb liquid. In which case the idols presumably smelt foul after a couple of days. Others suspected it was a giant hoax – someone could have been concealed at the other end of a long straw, sucking hard. Still others wondered whether something supernatural really was happening. What struck me was that this so-called miracle was utterly pointless, even cruel. Poor families who needed the protein and calcium in their limited supplies of milk, particularly to nourish children and the elderly, were giving it to idols that had no need of it at all. The miracles of the New Testament are quite different. Never gratuitous or sensation-seeking, Jesus' works of power are always demonstrations of the love of God in action.

There is a liquid flow in Christian faith. Not from us to God, like milk to elephant idols, but a double liquid flow from God to us. First the blood, then the river. First the death of Christ, to cleanse us from every stain of sin, and then the river of the Holy Spirit, bringing the life and love of God wherever the Spirit flows.

As for us, living the other side of the glorification of Christ at the cross, these promises now apply without any more need for delay. First we must be born again, putting our trust in the crucified Saviour. Then we can claim the promise of Jesus: the Holy Spirit is freely available to all who have put their trust in Christ. In John 7 we have Jesus' own explanation of how this promise can be fulfilled in his followers' lives: we must be thirsty, we must come, and then we must drink.

First, we must be thirsty

I was in Jerusalem once during a heatwave, and my guide kept insisting that we stop for another drink of water. I quizzed him and he explained the problem: 'Northern Europeans are not used to this kind of heat. You don't realize how much liquid you need to consume. And as you begin to dehydrate, you become weary and even less inclined to drink. The more you lose your thirst, the more trouble you are in.'

We can lose our thirst through bad teaching. Sometimes Christians are taught to avoid any mention of the Holy Spirit. Maybe we have been put off by another church in town that is too wacky for our taste. But the correct response to abuse is not disuse, but right use. Our attitude to the Holy Spirit and our understanding of his work must be shaped by the Bible, not by our individual experiences, good or bad.

Sometimes we're not deliberately avoiding the Spirit, but we think it would be a bad witness to acknowledge any kind of spiritual need. We become macho Christians, running on empty but never telling anyone how dry we have become. Confident that we received the Spirit when we became believers, we behave as if God has given us a single drop of his Spirit which is meant to last a lifetime. The trouble is that if we deny our spiritual thirst often enough, we desensitize ourselves until we find it hard to recognize how spiritually thirsty we really have become.

There are several other ways to lose our spiritual thirst. We can set our heart on other things and lose our appetite for God. We can get onto a treadmill of being too busy and not having any space left for God. We can be so busy giving that we have no time left to receive. I know these problems are real, because at times in my Christian life I have experienced each one of them.

Jesus certainly did not say, 'If anyone is thirsty, they should repent.' The problem is not being thirsty, it's lack of thirst. When we are not thirsty for God, the best thing we can do is to ask God to put salt on our spirit, quickening a new thirst within us for spiritual vitality that only the Holy Spirit can satisfy. What Jesus is saying can be put like this: 'If anyone is thirsty, have I got good news for you!'

Second, we must come to Jesus

Many people are frightened of God. This should come as no surprise, since God is so much more powerful than we are. In the Bible, whenever angels appear, the first thing they say is usually, 'Fear not.' Similarly, Jesus' resurrection appearances often begin by addressing fears and offering the peace of God.

The nearest most of us come to an angelic visitation is a school nativity play. Ten-year-old girls in ballet dresses adorned with tinsel parade onto the stage, accompanied by parental purrs of approval and cries of, 'Aren't they lovely?' There is, however, no recorded instance in the Bible of an angelic visitation being interrupted by someone exclaiming to the angel, 'I hope you don't mind my saying so, but you are looking absolutely lovely today!'

The reason why angels say 'Fear not' is that they are messengers of God, but their message will not get through if someone is paralysed with fear. The fear must be dealt with first. In Jesus' teaching on the Spirit, he reassured his followers that God would only give good gifts to his children and never play tricks on them. Above all, we can take comfort from this invitation to come to Jesus. No one could be more reliable and trustworthy than Jesus. In the Gospels, Jesus responds to every individual in a way that is tailor-made, with a perfect, personalized precision. There's no standardization with Jesus – he always knows the very best way of dealing with each individual, according to our temperament, circumstances and needs. We can bring our fears, and he'll deal with them first. We can let our defences down, because Jesus is supremely trustworthy.

Some Christians develop a 'Mr Anointed' mentality. If only they can receive prayer from a special 'mighty man of God', they will receive the Spirit in power. Please notice that Jesus did not say we should go to the apostles, or even to a particular meeting. He simply told us to come to him. Jesus alone can pour out the Spirit upon us, and on him alone we need to learn to depend.

Other Christians become preoccupied with techniques. I remember speaking at one conference in Germany where the organizers were surprised that my way of praying for people was so laid back. 'When we pray for someone,' they explained, 'we concentrate 100 per cent upon that individual, putting all our energy into the prayer. But when you pray you seem quite relaxed; you keep your eyes open and look around the room.'

If they had prayed for me with so much intensity, quite honestly it would have put me off and made it harder for me to respond to God. The reason I am relaxed in prayer is that I cannot do very much. All I am really doing is assisting in a moment of meeting between an individual and God. What happens next is between them and out of my hands. I pray with open eyes so that I can see how the individual is responding to prayer: a blank face, a yawn, a smile, tears or other reactions all give indications of what may be happening in someone's inner being. And I look around the room just to make sure there's nothing untoward happening that needs pastoral supervision.

As far as I can see, the great secret of techniques in prayer ministry is that we have to learn not to try too hard. We don't need to get hung up about praying in just the same way as someone else. And the most important thing is to get out of God's way. If we make too much effort or get bogged down in elaborate techniques, the most likely result is that our over-the-top way of praying becomes a distraction from real encounter with God.

Jesus certainly did not tell us always to go to the latest 'big name preacher' or even our local minister in order to receive effective personal prayer. He did not spell out a standardized prayer technique. Nor did he detail how we would react when he answers our prayer and pours out his Spirit. Some Christians become obsessed with side effects and outward reactions, whether joyful or sad, emotional or physical. Such reactions should not surprise us. We are made as integrated beings, experiencing life in an interconnected way, physically, emotionally and spiritually. If we become over-stressed, for example, we may experience headaches, sore shoulders, high blood pressure or chest pains, and we may also find it hard to pray. Likewise, if the Holy Spirit meets with us deeply, it should not surprise us if there are emotional or physical reactions. But these things are never standardized. We all react to events and experiences that touch us deeply on the inside, but in very different and personal ways.

There are therefore two extremes to avoid. The person who is seeking particular side effects needs to recover biblical priorities and learn to seek only Christ. The person who wants to come to Christ so long as there are no side effects at all must learn to seek Christ with no strings attached, and leave any emotional and physical reactions to the discretion of the Master. Jesus neither encouraged us to seek secondary things, nor guaranteed that they would never happen. He simply encouraged us to come to him, and that is precisely what we need to do.

Third, we must drink

Imagine that Claire, my wife, wakes me up in the middle of the night. 'Rob,' she croaks, 'I've a raging sore throat. Please go down to the kitchen and get me a glass of water.' I go to the kitchen, pick up a glass and then notice that it's dirty. Perhaps it's something to do with hard water, or even with the happy knowledge we have in London that every time we drink some tap water it has already been drunk by about 35 other people! Well, if the glass is dirty, I wash it. In the same way, if we come to Jesus to be filled with the Holy Spirit, when our lives are soiled we must be made clean before we can be filled. First the blood, then the river. First repentance, then a new filling with the Spirit of holiness.

I take the glass of water back to our bedroom, place it on Claire's bedside table and slump back into sleep. Half an hour later she wakes me again. 'Rob,' she croaks, 'I've a raging sore throat. Please go down to the kitchen and get me a glass of water.' I look to her side of the bed and see the first glass of water is still there, untouched. And so I say, '*Darling*, perhaps you'd like to drink that glassful first!'

We have to move from theory to practice. We must not only acknowledge our need, we must then come to Jesus for our need to be met. Perhaps you have met the kind of Christian who recognizes their need for more of God, but then does nothing but repeat a complaint, 'I'm so thirsty!' Jesus explains that we must come to him in receiving mode.

It's very hard to drink and talk at the same time. In the same way, it's very hard to receive of the Holy Spirit if we never stop talking to God. To drink means that we must lay down our defences, and that includes using spoken prayer as something to hide behind. The only way to drink is to come to Jesus in openness and surrender.

Jesus completes this teaching on receiving the Spirit by telling us what will happen as a result, promising that out of our inmost being will flow rivers of living water. Remember the telling detail in Ezekiel's vision: wherever the river flows, it brings life. The river of God flows into us, renewing our life on the inside. And then the river flows out of us, making us instruments of God's love to others. God blesses us in order to make us a blessing to many.

There is a familiar image in many cartoons of cowboys and indians. The indians let loose their arrows which soar through the sky and hit their target. The wounded cowboy staggers into hiding among some rocks. The indians can't find him and ride off. In order to treat his injuries, he pulls out the arrows one by one. When the last one has been removed, he has a drink of water and then, since this is a cartoon, the water pours out of all the holes where the arrows had pierced him.

Such craziness is typical of the world of cartoons, but it also illustrates Jesus' promise. We receive in order to give away. If we want to receive like a cuckoo in the nest – 'Bless me, just me, only for me!' – we completely miss the point of Jesus' teaching. We drink so that others might receive. We seek God's blessing not simply for our own sakes, but in order to become a blessing to many. The more we receive, the more others can be blessed.

There is one final detail in Jesus' invitation to receive the Spirit that we cannot afford to miss. All the verbs are in the present continuous tense. That means we could translate them like this: Whenever you become thirsty, come to me again, and drink again, and out of your inmost being will flow once more the streams of living water.

This is not a passage which only applies on one occasion in our Christian lives. We cannot put a tick in the margin of our Bible: been there, done that, got the testimony. Every day that we live this side of heaven, this passage continues to apply. The river of God is newly available to each of us this very day, if only we will take Jesus at his word.

As well as applying throughout our lives, this passage also has wonderful relevance on the day of our baptism. Just as we are immersed in water as we surrender ourselves into the arms of our fellow believers, we can be immersed in the Holy Spirit as we surrender ourselves into the arms of Jesus. I don't want you to miss out on the privilege of water baptism. Even more, I long for you to share in the fulfilment of Jesus' glorious promise as he pours out upon his followers the life-giving waters of the Spirit of God.

All we have to do is follow these simple steps, whether we are taking Jesus at his word for the first or thousandth time:

1. *Acknowledge* our spiritual thirst.
2. *Come to Jesus*, making his promise our own.
3. *Drink* as Jesus provides, opening our hearts in willing surrender.
4. *Enjoy the free flow of the streams of living water,* so that we become a blessing to others as Jesus blesses us.

The Spirit is the gracious gift of the Father and Son, available without limit to every believer. Come to Jesus, because he longs to lavish upon you the life-enriching abundance of the Holy Spirit.

Appendix 1

Two Weeks of Bible Readings on Baptism

1. Jesus' baptism   Matthew 3:13–17

2. Jesus' teaching on baptism   Matthew 28:16–20

3. Peter's teaching on baptism   Acts 2:32–39

4. Every believer baptized   Acts 2:40–47

5. A spiritual bath   Acts 22:6–16

6. A spiritual burial   Romans 6:1–11

7. A change of clothes   Colossians 3:5–14

8. Belonging   1 John 3:16–24

9. Adoption by the Father   Romans 8:15–17

10. Union with the Son   2 Corinthians 5:17–21

11. Receiving the Spirit   John 7:37–39

12. Confessing Christ   Romans 10:9–13

13. Assurance of salvation   1 John 1:5–2: 2

14. Pressing on   Hebrews 12:1–11

Appendix 2

Further Reading and Listening

You can follow up themes from this book in Rob's other writings, available from all good Christian bookshops.

Alive in the Spirit (The person and work of the Holy Spirit)
I Believe in Discipleship
Praying with Jesus (The Lord's Prayer and communion)
Prepare for Revival
The Sermon on the Mount
The Ten Commandments and the Decline of the West
21st-Century Church
Walking with God (Exploring prayer)

Many of Rob's teaching tapes can be ordered from his church's web site – www.kairos.org.uk

You can hear Rob regularly on Premier Radio – on medium wave in the London area (1305/1332/1413 khz) and worldwide on the web.

Rob has produced a leaflet on baptism to accompany this book which can be ordered from the Kairos web site. You can either purchase an individual copy or place a bulk order for your church.